WAITING

FOR

DEATH

THE PHILOSOPHICAL SIGNIFICANCE

OF BECKETT'S

EN ATTENDANT GODOT

Ramona Cormier

AND

Janis L. Pallister

THE UNIVERSITY OF ALABAMA PRESS

University, Alabama

To T.

SECOND PRINTING 1980

Library of Congress Cataloging in Publication Data

Cormier, Ramona, 1923–
   Waiting for death.

   Bibliography: p.
   Includes index.
   1. Beckett, Samuel, 1906–   En attendant
Godot. I. Pallister, Janis L., joint author.
II. Title.
PQ2603.E378E634   1979   842'.9'14   76-10218

CONTENTS

ACKNOWLEDGMENTS

The authors acknowledge with gratitude the assistance of the following in the preparation of this work: Paul Christianson of the Department of English of Wooster College, Lenita Locey and Michael Locey of the Department of Romance Languages of Bowling Green State University, and Donald Scherer and Peter Spader of the Department of Philosophy of Bowling Green State University. The authors are also grateful to Bowling Green State University for a grant that made possible an article appearing in *L'Esprit Créateur* (Fall 1971), which ultimately became chapter 6 herein, and to Miss Sandra Dauer, who typed the manuscript.

The authors also acknowledge with gratitude permission to quote from the copyrighted English and French versions of *En attendant Godot*, as follows:

Acknowledgment is also made to the periodical *L'Esprit Créateur*, in which portions of chapter six of the present work made their first appearance in print.

INTRODUCTION

The purpose of this study is twofold. First, our intention is to eval-
uate the deluge of critical opinions concerning Samuel Beckett's *En
attendant Godot* and through a careful analysis of the text to establish what appear to be the most satisfactory among these many
opinions. Second, and more important, we are concerned with ex-
tracting from this play the 'world view' of Beckett. However, taking
our cue from Beckett's own view that explanation of an art work in
terms extrinsic to itself seems ruled out as a valid critical approach,[1]
we do not see the task of evaluating Beckett's world view as involving a comparison of Beckett with philosophers *per se*, though
we will provide some commentary on this subject.[2] Furthermore,
our conviction is that one cannot arrive at a full appreciation of the
play until the true nature of this world view has been exposed. It
is, then, these two interrelated undertakings—the evaluation of
existing criticism with close reference to the text and the exposure
of Beckett's world view as it emerges through a literary and ideological analysis of the play—that we hope to accomplish. We realize, of course, that in our approach to these problems we may be
accused of committing the fallacy of attributing to the author intentions that in reality may not exist, but we consider this risk worth-
while and hope that the results of the investigation will be found
useful enough to outweigh any negative criticisms that might be
brought to bear against our particular point of departure.

A recurring theme in Beckett's works is the suggestion that the
source of man's troubles lies in his being born, and the very fact of

his birth means that he must atone for this birth and that he must cope with his existence, both on physical and mental planes.[3] The irony of this fate is that he is incapable of so doing, from external as well as internal factors, both of which point to man's finitude. All literary as well as philosophical ramifications of Beckett's writings appear to stem from this notion of the finite condition of man, who is not so much tragic as he is absurd, even ridiculous, because, in his efforts to overcome the fundamental anguish of his existence, he uses faulty equipment, resulting in a series of paradoxes. Where he seeks independence, his dependency becomes still more acute. Where he strives for rational explanations, the inadequacy of his reason hinders him. When he tries to communicate he fails. All efforts at systemization fall into disorder. His memory, which entails his sense of time and identity, is defective and chaotic. His body, the vehicle of these activities, is not only unreliable and in a state of constant decomposition but even makes demands upon him that interfere with his effectiveness. Social institutions, products of his own faulty nature, are no better as mechanisms for dealing with the problems with which his life confronts him. Suicide would be the only logical solution, and yet this is apparently not an alternative. Rather, man must continue to play the games that fill the emptiness of his existence until he is finally overcome by death. There is "nothing to be done" except to give himself the illusion, in one way or another, that he is "doing something." "Doing something" generates habit, one of the sources of man's boredom and of his inability to change his pattern of behavior. These meaningless activities may also give rise to false hope, which in its turn feeds habit. Due to these limitations, tedium and deterioration are the insurmountable lot of man. He is hopelessly trapped.

All of the foregoing elements are to be found in *En attendant Godot*, a play that can be considered focal in the work of Beckett. The four characters of the play are involved in situations that are devised to cope with "what to do." But these games and situations ultimately serve only to illustrate the futility and the inefficacy of such efforts. The four men reach an impasse, not only because of the faulty nature of their tools, but also because of the ineffectiveness of the by-products of these tools. In dealing with their physical and social environment, these characters demonstrate the conflicts between body and mind and point up the inadequacies of reason, the senses, memory, and all the extensions of these mechanisms as they are found in societal behavior.

Although these notions of impotence and deterioration are manifest in all four characters, in Vladimir the emphasis is on the limitations of the intellect; in Estragon it is on the restricting demands of the body; while in the tyrannical Pozzo and the submissive Lucky the emphasis is on the social degeneracy produced by this kind of relationship. In addition, while each of the characters makes an effort to cope with the problems of past, present, and future, Estragon confines himself largely to the contingencies of the present, demonstrating memory lapses in terms of both the past and the future, while Vladimir grapples with problems concerning the past (the two thieves) and operates more than Estragon in terms of the future ("on attend Godot"). Pozzo measures time but is hostile to its concept (p. 104), and Lucky makes faltering attempts to situate the content of his speech in a historical context ("depuis la mort de Voltaire"). Furthermore, the characters, paired as they are, provide the theme of interdependence (another type of limitation), which is in conflict with the urge of each of them to be independent. The interdependence of the characters, however, does not rule out the basic solitude of each, nor the failure of communication, which is everywhere present in the play, in the breakdown in conversation as well as in the chaotic nature of the language. Suicide as one of the ways of escaping boredom is suggested by Estragon and entertained by Vladimir, but it is finally rejected on the basis of their interdependence and also on the basis of their incapacity to succeed at it as well as their failure to possess the necessary instruments. It seems that the characters must await death, which will bring an end to the tedium and meaninglessness of their existence. Only then can the game stop and the waiting for Godot cease.

In order to convey this view of the limitations of man and his products, Beckett has seen fit to abandon conventional dramatic forms. His antiplay, a diptych containing a play-within-a-play, has no characterization and no traditional plot. The fusion of genres and the disparate sources of the work provide an appropriate vehicle for his fragmented and prismatic view of the universe. Beckett's pessimistic concept of man has certain points in common with some existentialist philosophers, but, unlike them, he does not propose a means for coping with the meaninglessness of existence. *En attendant Godot* is not a morality play.[4] It is not a play with a message. It is, rather, a presentation of a world view that concentrates upon the tedium and absurdity that envelop life, and this presentation is at once similar to and different from an assertion of the same world view by a philosopher.

1

THE CHARACTERS

Gunther Anders in "Being Without Time"[1] argues that the characters in *En attendant Godot* are "abstractions" and that Estragon and Vladimir are men in general performing in a nonworld. It seems more accurate to say that the play's four characters, taken together, portray universal man as he confronts the world we live in, not as he deals with a "nonworld." These characters are not abstractions but, rather, the embodiments of abstract principles. Simply on the basis of their names, drawn from four different countries or languages, mirroring the east and the west, the south and the north, and to some extent even suggesting their condition in life, one can argue that all four characters must be included for the play to be understood in terms of man in general.[2]

But the case for universal man is even more clearly shown in the various levels of human existence—metaphysical, sociological, and psychological—that are reflected in the positions the characters occupy. Universal man as portrayed by Beckett is a finite being. For this reason Beckett emphasizes the limitations and paradoxes that occur at each of these levels. It goes without saying, of course, that because his nihilistic view is a distorted one, showing man only at his worst, Beckett has in the strictest sense failed to portray universal man.

In this play the metaphysical level is represented by the mind/body duality.[3] Clearly, Beckett's intention is to demonstrate through this duality the limitations of the mind and body taken separately or together.

But the mind/body duality is not the only metaphysical consideration dealt with in the play. There are also the paradoxes arising from man's conflicting desires for solitude and society. Furthermore, the play suggests that the restrictions brought about by the mind/body dichotomy and by these conflicting desires result in failure at the sociological and psychological levels. Thus, at every level man's limitations are depicted as insurmountable and his existence as very bleak indeed.

These three levels, with their accompanying paradoxes and limitations, are represented variously by one pair of characters (Vladimir and Estragon) or the other (Pozzo and Lucky) or by an interaction of the two pairs.[4] While there is a certain amount of overlapping, the Vladimir-Estragon pair exemplifies on the metaphysical level the seeming duality of man's nature, and the Pozzo-Lucky pair depicts man's activities and relationships on the social level. Yet both pairs embody such metaphysical problems as the conflicting desires for solitude and society, and both exemplify certain psychological and sociological failings, and, by extension, failures.

Viewing the mind/body dichotomy as it specifically appears in the play reveals that, though both Vladimir and Estragon have bodily afflictions, Vladimir is an intellectual who operates primarily in terms of the past and the future, whereas Estragon is more concerned with creature comforts that link him to the present.[5] Vladimir reflects upon a historical problem having moral and theological implications; Estragon, failing to grasp the enormity of the problem, dismisses it with the cynical statement, "Les gens sont des cons" (p. 15). (His statement, much weaker in English, tags humanity as a bunch of bloody, ignorant apes [p. 9A].) Again, as Vladimir puzzles over whether it is indeed Saturday, Estragon falls asleep. Estragon is a more egoistical person than Vladimir. Furthermore, he seeks to gratify his appetites, and he readily responds to sensory experience. Although his memory is usually very faulty, he has no trouble remembering the pleasant (colored maps) and the unpleasant (his beatings, Lucky's kick). It is Estragon who eats but Vladimir, a father figure, who provides the food. The two are in further contrast in that Vladimir is concerned with moral issues and Estragon is not. Upon seeing Lucky's condition, for example, Vladimir

exclaims that it's a scandal (p. 31). Moral issues do not interest Estragon, who seeks materialistic gains or sensual gratification in practically everything: he wants Pozzo's bones; he thinks he may get
money if he tarries for Pozzo, who says that he will not regret having
waited (p. 33); he would take a *louis* or even *cent sous* in recom-
pense for the boredom Pozzo has cost him (p. 45); he hopes to get
more bones for picking Pozzo up (p. 90). Estragon has trouble with
his shoes; Vladimir, with his hat. Vladimir's body odors issue from
his mouth, Estragon's from his feet. Vladimir wants Lucky to think;
Estragon wants him to dance. This difference in perspective manifests itself in the fact that Estragon, the more sensual of the two,
has been a poet,[6] while Vladimir, the more intellectual, tends to
be a philosopher. Vladimir's apparent concern with the rational
leads him to refuse to listen to Estragon's dreams. On the other
hand, Estragon, who challenges the capabilities of Vladimir's reason
by asking him whether it is really Saturday and not Sunday, Mon-
day, or Friday (p. 17), is unmoved by the very problems he raises,
which ultimately appear to him to be trivial and hairsplitting. Since
both characters are possessed of a body and a mind, it would be
extreme to say that Vladimir represents exclusively the mind and
Estragon exclusively the body. Nevertheless, in Vladimir the emphasis is on the intellectual, and in Estragon the emphasis is on the
affective and the physical.[7]

Furthermore, the limitations and deteriorations of mind and body
can be witnessed in the two characters. Both have intellectual deficiencies and both are sexually impotent. The play suggests that
rational conclusions which we normally accept unquestioningly can
be the subject of skepticism; for when challenged by the less rational of the two bums, the more rational one is unable to substantiate
what day of the week it is. Estragon momentarily shakes Vladimir's
belief that it is evening by proposing that it might rather be dawn,
to which Vladimir replies that Estragon should not say foolish things
because the west is over there; whereupon Estragon asks Vladimir
what he knows about the matter (p. 98). In addition, Estragon
points out to Vladimir his faulty reasoning in the following passage:

Estragon: C'est curieux, plus on va, moins c'est bon.
Vladimir: Pour moi c'est le contraire.

Estragon: C'est-à-dire?
Vladimir: Je me fais au goût au fur et à mesure.
Estragon (ayant longuement réfléchi): C'est ça le contraire? (p. 24)[8]

Moreover, Vladimir is unable to explain to his own satisfaction why
some believe Luke's account of the two thieves in preference to the
other three Gospels, one of which is at variance with this story and
two of which omit it. On the other hand, despite the fact that Estragon can on occasion point out these limitations of the mind to
Vladimir, he is unable to remember what has happened in either
the remote or the immediate past and must constantly have things
recalled to him by Vladimir. Vladimir also confuses Estragon in
matters of color perception. In the second act Estragon cannot remember whether his shoes were black or grey or whether the new
ones are yellow or of a greenish cast. He is like a child clinging to
his father's coattail when he hears the approaching steps of Lucky
and Pozzo. In the second act he behaves irrationally and even admits that he has "lost his head" (p. 85, ll. 23–25).

But the body, the keeper of the mind, is no less subject to limitation and deterioration. Both men are sexually impotent.[9] In keeping with their respective focuses, Estragon suffers from foot trouble,
while Vladimir complains that his hat causes his head to hurt. Vladimir's advanced age is accompanied by a prostate condition that
makes it difficult for him to laugh; he must restrict himself to smiling
(p. 12). His prostate trouble also makes it necessary for him to in-
terrupt conversations and leave the scene from time to time—a
source of amusement for Estragon. The physical debility of both
men is further shown by their inability to sustain their calisthenic
exercises as a way of killing time (p. 87). The cycle of alimentation-
elimination, another physical impasse often noted by Beckett's critics, is reflected by Estragon's frequent need to eat (he eats twice
in the course of this short play and would a third time if the radishes
were of the right kind) and by Vladimir's frequent need to urinate
(he leaves the scene several times for this purpose, while Estragon
never does).

The inability to maintain one's equilibrium is another very basic
and yet more complex physical function that is a recurring theme
in the play. When Estragon goes to show Vladimir his sore leg he
almost falls twice (p. 77). Estragon stumbles when imitating Lucky's

dance (p. 47), and Vladimir and Estragon both stumble when they hold up Lucky (p. 54). Estragon falls down when he is rushing to hide himself (p. 85), and both fall down when they try to help Pozzo get up. Both Estragon and Vladimir stumble at various points in the play (e.g., p. 87, where Vladimir has proposed an exercise for recovering their equilibrium).[10]

Physical pain, a major cause of limitation as well as of distraction and the source of much human suffering, is frequently endured by both Vladimir and Estragon. Pain occurs when Vladimir tries to laugh; it is experienced by Estragon when he is beaten during the night and when he is kicked by Lucky. But perhaps the most terrible thing is something quite different; namely, to have thought ("Ce qui est terrible c'est d'avoir pensé" [p. 74].). It is conceivable, then, that thought, which can cause one to remember pain and to imagine death—the end of both body and mind—is more painful than anything the body independent of the mind might be called upon to bear.

Insofar as the mind/body dichotomy is concerned, and as Vladimir himself seems to sense when he says that he will take the part of Lucky and Estragon that of Pozzo (p. 83), there are definite parallels between Vladimir and Lucky and between Estragon and Pozzo.

Lucky is not a porter (pp. 30, 36) but rather a teacher or philosopher of sorts, who has taught Pozzo everything he knows (p. 38). All four characters wear hats, but Lucky, like Vladimir, wears one that seems to be peculiarly connected with the intellectual processes. However, the limitations of mind to be seen in Vladimir are infinitely greater in Lucky. Without his hat, he is literally unable to think (p. 50). He must be ordered to think (p. 51) and will do so only then. And when he is ordered to think by Pozzo, his demented thoughts revolve around disorganized bits of knowledge drawn from different fields of learning (science, sports, literature, theology, etc.), his sentences are fragmented, and his speech is halting. Ironically, the content of his long speech is intended to demonstrate the physical and mental deterioration of man, rather than his progress in these fields.

On the other hand, Pozzo has many affinities with Estragon. Like Estragon, he is physically oriented. He eats and drinks, while Lucky waits upon his physical needs. While all of the characters are

egoistical, Pozzo, like Estragon, has this as a salient feature of his
personality. (On page 25 he asks if his name is not meaningful to
them and he claims to be of divine origin; on page 27 he regrets
that the road through his property belongs to everyone; on page 28
while he recognizes Vladimir and Estragon to be human beings like
himself, he finds that they resemble him only imperfectly; on page
35 he enjoys being in the limelight and insists upon being listened
to; on page 94 Vladimir claims that Pozzo thinks only of himself.)
He manages to divert sympathy directed to Lucky so that it is re-
directed toward him (p. 39). Also, like Estragon, Pozzo has a very
faulty memory. He cannot remember Godot's name (pp. 33, 42).[11]
He is constantly misplacing his many possessions. He loses his pipe
(p. 40), his throat spray (p. 47), his watch, which, ironically, was a
souvenir from his grandfather (p. 55). He forgets his folding chair
and has to go back after it (p. 57). He even admits that he has a
faulty memory: "C'est que ma mémoire est défectueuse" (p. 45).
He repeatedly loses track of his line of thought and repeatedly asks
to be reminded of what he was saying.

Physical pain is endured by both Lucky and Pozzo—by Lucky
through Pozzo (throughout Act I) and through Estragon and Vladimir, who kick him repeatedly to get him to respond (pp. 102–03),
and by Pozzo at the hands of Vladimir (p. 95). In addition, the physical deterioration of Pozzo and Lucky, like Pozzo's faulty memory
and the limitations of Lucky's intellect, is more drastic than is the
case with Estragon and Vladimir. In Act II Pozzo is blind (that is,
though predominantly a physical being, he has no visual perception), while Lucky is mute (that is, though predominantly a thinking
being, he cannot express his ideas). The theme of disequilibrium
is also intensified, for at one point all four characters are on the
ground, and Pozzo cannot get up without assistance (pp. 88–94).
Indeed, physical abuse, physical deterioration, and physical disequilibrium have reached their extreme limits by the end of the
play.

Despite similarities between the two pairs, similarities that revolve around the mind/body dichotomy, Lucky and Pozzo have profound significance independent of Estragon and Vladimir on the
sociological level. Critics have often stated that their presence in
the play constitutes a play-within-a-play,[12] a notion that can be sub-

stantiated by Pozzo's statement concerning the reversal of roles (p. 36, ll. 23–25) and by his desire to be praised following his speech about the night (p. 44). In terms of Beckett's world view, however, Lucky and Pozzo do not simply constitute a play-within-a-play; they do not simply echo the mind/body dichotomy seen in Estragon and Vladimir; they have independent meaning on several social (i.e., political, religious, and ethical) levels. These manifestations of society, which are already decadent at the appearance of Pozzo and Lucky, continue their deterioration throughout the course of the play. They reflect the theme of solitude versus community and the related theme of dependence versus independence, both of which appear with Vladimir and Estragon and which occur in the interaction of the two pairs. At this point the metaphysical and sociological levels fuse completely.

Politically speaking, Pozzo and Lucky represent the tyrant and the slave. Pozzo, embodying the authority associated with the head of government, is an affluent property owner. It is he who owns the land adjacent to the road where Vladimir and Estragon await Godot. This affluence is also reflected in his many possessions, all of which constitute a heavy burden in that he must keep track of them and have assistance in transporting them from place to place. It is, of course, Lucky who fulfills the role of porter even though he is not equal to the task; this is not his real trade ("En réalité, il porte comme un porc. Ce n'est pas son métier" [p. 36].). In such a political situation as this, where one has willfully accepted the position of the unquestioning slave (p. 35), one is obviously not free to practice one's real trade. Further evidence of Pozzo's affluence and tyranny can be found in the fact that he eats and drinks well, throwing nothing but the bones to Lucky.

The verbal and physical abuse to which Pozzo subjects Lucky, a treatment that Pozzo himself recognizes as being inhuman (p. 33), has resulted in Lucky's dehumanization, in his being deprived of every scrap of dignity, even that commonly given an animal. In contrast to Lucky, Pozzo is extremely concerned with his dignity and wonders how he will be able to sit down again, naturally and without seeming to bend (p. 32). Self-important and authoritarian, perhaps even drunk with power, Pozzo insists upon being heard by an audience whose attentions are undivided. He wants to know whether everyone is present and looking at him, as he doesn't like to talk in a vacuum (p. 35). Like many a political personality, he gives a speech that appears to bore Estragon and Vladimir. He is full of platitudes pertaining to being able to learn something from anyone ("Plus je rencontre de gens, plus je suis heureux. Avec la moindre créature on s'instruit, on s'enrichit, on goûte mieux son bonheur" [pp. 33–34].), and to the idea that life is a veil of tears ("Les larmes du monde sont immuables. Pour chacun qui se met à pleurer, quelque part un autre s'arrête. Il en va de même du rire" [p. 38].). He is also full of empty rhetoric, priding himself on his orator's voice, which he protects and "inflates" with an atomizer. Yet he lacks enough in self-confidence that he requires encouragement and seeks praise for his delivery (p. 45). Much like a Roman emperor placating the populace, he offers to requite Estragon and Vladimir for listening to him by offering entertainment provided by his slave. Also very much like a monarch, he is extremely deferent, and it is he who hopes to profit from any encounter, whether he gives anything or not (pp. 33–34). It is possible, too, that his folding chair symbolizes a throne,[13] and his pipe and his whip can be viewed as his gavel and scepter, signs of his authority and wealth.

Perhaps the authoritarian nature of the relationship between Lucky and Pozzo also symbolizes the relationship between an orthodox priesthood and the faithful. Pozzo points out that he is of divine origin (p. 26). His accoutrements, which have been mentioned in connection with the political aspects of the Lucky-Pozzo duo, are also suggestive of religious ritual. Pozzo puts on and takes off his coat much as a priest does his vestments, with Lucky acting as a kind of server. His folding chair is like a cathedra, and his efforts at dignity in sitting down and getting up hint at formalized practices in religious services. The pipe and the whip could be symbolic of the rod and the staff (the crozier) of the pastor. Again with Lucky acting as a kind of server, Pozzo partakes of a ritualistic meal of bread, wine, and fowl that suggests the Eucharist. He eats and drinks alone, throwing only the scraps to Lucky, or, as it turns out in Act I, to Estragon. On the other hand, Lucky manifests the characteristics of a certain element of the faithful, thinking and acting only when and as authority commands. The thought of separation, like a fear of excommunication, reduces Lucky to tears (pp. 36–37). Lucky, in his obedience to authority, has replaced habitual thought patterns with the habit of not thinking, so that when he is required to revive his habits of thought and speech he can utter only scraps of thought in incoherent language. Similarly, when asked to dance, his movements are stiff and ungraceful; that is, his body, used to being bent by heavy burdens, is unable to move freely. The habits of thought and motion, then, have been replaced by new habits of disuse. How has this come about? Seemingly, the metaphysical relationship of mind and body has been brought under the control of a sociological force. And yet it could be, as Lucky's name implies, that he is close to the states of absolute silence and immobility that are ideals to the nihilist—that in terms of the play Lucky is truly lucky and that his name is not to be understood ironically.

The symbols of authority associated with Pozzo (and particularly the seat) are all portable, which suggests that traditional seats of authority, ecclesiastical and secular, are now decadent, that is, no longer well rooted. Vestiges of this kind of authority thus appear to go more with the person who has assumed headship than with the institution itself. In other words, the rise and fall of the institution appear to depend here more on the individual than on the recognized validity of the architecturally frozen arena of government or church.

To pursue the issues of decadence and servitude, if in Act I the relationship between Pozzo and Lucky is one that horrifies Vladimir (and Estragon?), not to mention the spectator, in Act II the situation becomes even more horrible; what was seen as being already in a state of decadence has reached an even greater degree of debasement. Pozzo is now blind and Lucky mute. In Act I they had a destination (though Lucky's was not a happy one); in Act II they wander aimlessly from place to place. Lucky could now feasibly sever his ties with the despotic Pozzo, but once again long-standing habit has made this impossible. Lucky continues to follow orders (p. 103), though he appears to respond a bit less readily to them now and must be kicked out of his sleep and made to act.

Turning to the question of solitude and community and to that of dependence and independence, the heart of the play *En attend-*

ant Godot is not in the characteristics of Estragon, Vladimir, Pozzo, or Lucky taken individually but, rather, in their interaction. Although each one (with the possible exception of Lucky) may manifest the desire to be independent of the other, independence is only an illusion. Furthermore, and ironically, although each may wish to be independent, none wishes to suffer the consequences of absolute independence (if indeed such a thing were possible), for under these conditions the character would lose what identity he has, an identity that hinges on his fundamental quality of being a social animal. Total independence, however ideal it may be in the sense that it leads to absolute negations of language and other social activities (absolutes that are desirable to the nihilist), is nevertheless an impossibility. Dependence, on the other hand, has serious drawbacks and limitations; so man perpetually fluctuates between his desire for an impossible independence and a too restrictive yet necessary dependence.

The nature of the relationship between Estragon and Vladimir is extrasocietal (or metaphysical).[14] Vladimir is to some extent more rational than Estragon, and Estragon more body-oriented than Vladimir. To the degree that the two characters can be made to fuse into a symbolic whole, not only is the mind/body dichotomy represented but also the fundamental interdependence and inseparability of mind and body.[15] And even though at times mind wishes to be independent of body and body wishes to be free of the reins of reason, the inseparability of Estragon and Vladimir serves to show that no such independence can be realized.

But to the degree that Vladimir and Estragon are distinct personalities—in fact, they are diametrically opposed—another type of interdependence, one that is of a societal nature but is not institutionalized, emerges: their friendship. This friendship, having qualities of ambivalence (p. 67) and latent homosexuality, is probably an illusion, but it is a necessary illusion. Vladimir needs Estragon to combat loneliness and to sustain certain types of games. Estragon needs Vladimir to protect him, to give him food, to help him take off his shoes; and he would like Vladimir to assume the role of father by listening to his dreams (a role that Vladimir refuses to accept in this particular case). Like Vladimir, he needs someone to help him pass the time, someone to play games with.[16]

Vladimir and Estragon are, then, tied to one another symbolically in several different ways, and their frequent discussions about separating (pp. 18, 63, 68) are motivated largely by a desire to give themselves the illusion that a separation is possible. And if indeed independence were possible, it could not be tolerated because the solitude resulting from such a separation would be unbearable (p. 17, Vladimir does not let Estragon sleep because he feels alone; p. 104, Vladimir wakes him up because he feels alone; p. 67, Estragon chides Vladimir because he left him alone; p. 79, together they find something to give them the impression that they exist).[17]

Yet Vladimir and Estragon, though existentially tied to one another, are extrasocietal because they are not tied to a particular place (p. 22), to historical time, or to one another in a literal sense. Are they tied to Godot? They say they are not and yet they seem to be, at least in the sense that they are waiting for him, and this, if not habit, seems to be the principal thing binding them to each other. They are hopelessly trapped. They have reached an impasse on this road, in which may be discerned a metaphor for life. They are caught is a situation in which they cannot separate from one another, or give up waiting for Godot, or leave the place in which they find themselves. They appear to be condemned to an inertia that can only end with death. The play ends with Vladimir's suggestion that they depart, but both of the characters remain immobile. Stasis is their lot.

The case of Lucky and Pozzo differs from that of Vladimir and Estragon in that, while they are also tied to one another symbolically, Lucky is literally tied to Pozzo, thus adding another dimension to the theme of imprisonment that runs through the play. Indeed, Lucky, thinking he is ensnared, can no longer dance anything except "The Net" (p. 47). A further difference is that the relationship of Lucky and Pozzo, though equally interdependent, is intrasocietal and institutional. Their interdependence is to be understood in terms of the roles given them by society, roles that are grounded in habit and inertia. The tyrant needs his slave(s),[18] the priest needs the faithful, the sadist needs the masochist, and vice versa. The play implies that once one of these roles is assumed there is no way to reverse it. In Act I, Pozzo maintains that he is going to Saint-Sauveur, where he will sell Lucky; yet in Act II he has not

only not sold Lucky, their interdependence has become the more
evident. Lucky now wants only Pozzo's consolation, not that of
Vladimir or Estragon (p. 37), and he seeks Pozzo's pity so that Pozzo
will renounce the idea of their separating (p. 36). Pozzo, in fact,
stresses their inseparability when he says "A vrai dire, chasser de
tels êtres, ce n'est pas possible. Pour bien faire, il faudrait les tuer"
(p. 37). ["The truth is you can't drive such creatures away. The best
thing would be to kill them."] The historical connection, of course,
further intensifies their interrelationship.

   While the interdependence of Vladimir and Estragon is to some
extent symbiotic, that of Pozzo and Lucky is clearly detrimental in
all respects. There are no signs of progress. On the contrary, already
degraded in Act I, in Act II they are leading an existence lacking
any direction or significance whatsoever. What was tottering on the
verge of collapse in the first act is crumbling in Act II. Each has lost
what power would be required to remedy the situation. Pozzo can
no longer see, Lucky can no longer speak,[19] and neither can sustain
himself for any length of time, nor can they help one another up
once they have fallen. They are condemned to wander about aimlessly, and if no one is near to help them when they fall they must
simply lie there until they are able to get up, however long this
may be. Apparently, once deterioration has set in at the institutional
level, no salvaging of the institution is possible.

   The interdependence of the two pairs of characters is echoed in
an interdependence that crosses over from one pair to the other.
That is, Vladimir and Estragon need Pozzo and Lucky because the
latter help the former to pass the time. Lucky, commanded by
Pozzo, provides Vladimir and Estragon with a divertissement. Furthermore, as Jacques Guicharnaud has pointed out, Lucky fulfills
the tragic role of the Western intellectual and artist[20] called upon
to perform for the uninvolved consumer, represented by Vladimir
and Estragon.[21] The arrival of Pozzo and Lucky in Act II constitutes
reenforcement and relief at a point when Vladimir and Estragon are
about to run out of games. Thus, again Pozzo and Lucky help to
pass the time; for Vladimir, upon seeing them again, is confident
that they will have something to do during the rest of the evening
("Voilà notre fin de soirée assurée" [p. 88]). Furthermore, in Act
II, the fallen Pozzo and Lucky provide an opportunity—whether

it is pursued or not—for Vladimir and Estragon to assert their humanity by performing a charitable act:

> Faisons quelque chose, pendant que l'occasion se présente! Ce n'est pas tous les jours qu'on a besoin de nous. Non pas à vrai dire qu'on ait précisément besoin de nous. D'autres feraient aussi bien l'affaire, sinon mieux. L'appel que nous venons d'entendre, c'est plutôt à l'humanité tout entière qu'il s'adresse. Mais à cet endroit, en ce moment, l'humanité c'est nous, que ça nous plaise ou non. Profitons-en, avant qu'il soit trop tard. Représentons dignement pour une fois l'engeance où le malheur nous a fourrés. Qu'en dis-tu? (p. 91)

> [Let us do something, while we have the chance! It is not every day that we are needed. Not indeed that we personally are needed. Others would meet the case equally well, if not better. To all mankind they were addressed, those cries for help still ringing in our ears! But at this place, at this moment of time, all mankind is us, whether we like it or not. Let us make the most of it, before it is too late! Let us represent worthily for once the foul brood to which a cruel fate consigned us! What do you say? (p. 51)]

Just as Vladimir and Estragon need Pozzo and Lucky, so also do Pozzo and Lucky need Vladimir and Estragon, Pozzo far more than Lucky. If Vladimir and Estragon require a divertissement, a divertissement implies spectators. It is evident from his question as to how they found his performance that Pozzo the orator requires a Vladimir and an Estragon (p. 44); and Lucky, the professor, the intellectual, and the performing artist, also demands an audience.

In addition, Pozzo hopes to gain from his encounter with Vladimir and Estragon; for, in his opinion one can learn from anyone ("Avec la moindre créature, on s'instruit, on s'enrichit, on goûte mieux son bonheur" [p. 32]). He believes this will be so, especially if Vladimir and Estragon are men, that is, his peers, for he does not seem to regard Lucky as a human being ("Vous êtes bien des êtres humains, cependant. A ce que je vois. De la même espèce que moi. De la même espèce que Pozzo! D'origine divine!" [p. 26].). Later on he says that the road is long when one travels alone without meeting a living soul (p. 27), thus showing at once that he does not consider Lucky to be human and that he needs Vladimir and Estragon to combat his loneliness. At other points he manifests this need for company, thanking them for having kept him company (p. 32); or begging them to tarry ("Restez encore un peu, vous ne le regretterez pas" [p. 33]), or complaining to them that he has difficulty leaving (p. 56).

Inasmuch as Pozzo and Lucky represent institutions in a state of decay, they require help from the outside, temporary though it may be, unsustaining though it may be, in order to rise again.[22] This is the potential function of Estragon and Vladimir, which they discuss at length and ultimately perform. Thus, the Pozzo-Lucky duet has substantial need of Vladimir and Estragon.

The theme of solitude is woven in and out of the recurrent themes of dependence and interdependence. So much do Vladimir and Estragon wish to ward off their loneliness that even in those acts that imply total solitude, especially that of suicide, they show themselves to be social creatures. Suicide is contemplated as a joint effort. Inversely, Vladimir, while singing to himself, chooses a song that implies group participation—he sings a round. This ambivalence regarding separation and solitude also occurs to a lesser degree in the relationship between Pozzo and Lucky. Thus, on the one hand, the characters, excluding Lucky, frequently express a desire to be independent of one another.[23] On the other hand, solitude is a thing that they consistently and paradoxically flee.

Still another dimension of the theme of finitude, seen not only in *En attendant Godot* but in many of Beckett's other works, is psychological abnormality.[24] The presence of this in the play provides the third level discussed earlier in the chapter and hinted at in the discussion of the interrelationships of the two pairs. This psychological level, which is tied to both of the other levels and which in its theme of the deterioration of the individual reflects what the theme of deterioration in society shows on a grander scale, is of sufficient magnitude to warrant special study at this time.

The world of *En attendant Godot* is a world from which women are absent, a sterile world, a world wherein there is departure from the natural and biological order. Vladimir, more than the other characters, can be called impotent on several scores. He himself views his sexual impotence as a desperate condition, for he sees in the act of hanging a way to get an erection or, in French, a "moyen de se bander" (p. 19), surely a futile and paradoxical outcome, since suicide, as it results in death, would obviate the sexual gratification called for by the erection. His impotence is a manifestation of his prostate trouble and his senility.[25] This prostate condition makes laughter difficult and painful for him; so he is forced to restrict himself to a smile only, while moving his hand to his pubis, with his facial expression contorted.

In view of his impotence, it is ironic indeed that Vladimir is a vestigial descendant of the ancient phallic clown Arlequino from the *commedia dell'arte* tradition. The carrot, which is used to show the father-son relationship of Estragon and Vladimir, can also be viewed as a symbol for the huge phallus always carried by Arlequino.[26] On the other hand, Estragon, to whom the carrot is proffered, is also, at least in part, one of the *commedia dell'arte zanni*, perhaps representing Pulcinello. It is not improbable that the carrot scene, not to mention other factors in the play, points to a latent homosexuality existing in the pair and that the ambivalence they manifest toward each other can be seen as emanating to some extent from this potential homosexuality. The following scene will illustrate this ambivalence, which, however, is evident in many other places and which occurs whenever the interdependence of the two men is in view:

Vladimir: Encore toi! . . . Viens que je t'embrasse!

Estragon: Ne me touche pas!

Vladimir: Veux-tu que je m'en aille? (*Un temps.*) Gogo! (*Un temps. Vladimir le regarde avec attention.*) On t'a battu? (*Un temps.*) Gogo! (*Estragon se tait toujours, la tête basse.*) Où as-tu passé la nuit? (*Silence. Vladimir avance.*)

*Estragon:*Ne me touche pas! Ne me demande rien! Ne me dis rien! Reste avec moi!

Vladimir: Est-ce je t'ai jamais quitté?

Estragon: Tu m'as laissé partir.

Vladimir: Regarde-moi! (*Estragon ne bouge pas. D'une voix tonnante.*) Regarde-moi, je te dis!

Estragon lève la tête. Ils se regardent longuement, en reculant, avançant et penchant la tête comme devant un objet d'art, tremblant de plus en plus l'un vers l'autre, puis soudain s'étreignent, en se tapant sur le dos. Fin de l'étreinte. Estragon, n'étant plus soutenu, manque de tomber. (p. 67)

[*Vladimir:* You again! Come here till I embrace you.
Estragon: Don't touch me!
Vladimir: Do you want me to go away? (*Pause.*) Gogo! (*Pause. Vladimir observes him attentively.*) Did they beat you? (*Pause.*) Gogo!
(*Estragon remains silent, head bowed.*) Where did you spend the
night?
Estragon: Don't touch me! Don't question me! Don't speak to me!
Stay with me!
Vladimir: Did I ever leave you?
Estragon: You let me go.
Vladimir: Look at me. (*Estragon does not raise his head. Violently.*)
Will you look at me! *Estragon raises his head. They look long at
each other, then suddenly embrace, clapping each other on the
back. End of the embrace. Estragon, no longer supported, almost
falls.* (pp. 37–38)]

The expression "nec tecum nec sine te," which Beckett uses in reference to Hamm and Clov, applies equally well to Estragon and
Vladimir. An identity problem also arises as a result of this complicated psychological arrangement, but this particular subject will
be discussed at a later point in the present study.

Estragon, too, exhibits abnormal patterns of behavior, chiefly
those of infantilism and voyeurism. He uses baby talk in telling
Vladimir why they should not commit suicide (p. 20). While he assumes a "posture utérine," he is sung to sleep by the lullaby of
Vladimir, the father figure (pp. 80–81), who also consoles him when
he awakens frightened from a bad dream (p. 81) and promises to
protect him in the event that Lucky should strike out against him
(p. 101). These are merely a few of the instances of Estragon's infantilism.[27] As for his voyeurism, it is apparent in the amusement
he derives from watching Vladimir when he goes off stage to urinate. He even enlists Pozzo, telling him to come and have a look
("Venez . . . venez . . . vite . . . Regardez" [p. 41]). Pozzo's "oh!
là là!" in response suggests that he too finds the scene pleasurable.
In contrast to the theme of voyeurism, subconscious exhibitionism
is to be seen both in Vladimir, who is careless about closing his fly
(p. 11), and in Estragon, whose trousers are down around his feet
at the end of the play.

Masochism and sadism also appear, particularly in the Lucky-Pozzo pair. The masochist needs a sadist and the sadist needs a masochist, of course, and to this end Lucky accepts unquestioningly the mental and physical whippings given to him by Pozzo. These flagellations, which have pietistic overtones, are a consequence of the master-slave or sadist-masochist complex. But Estragon, too, is beaten during the night by some unidentified party or parties (*ils*), suggesting, albeit somewhat loosely, that he too may be involved in some type of sadist-masochist relationship. (We say "loosely" because we recognize that a masochist usually knows who his tormentor is or was.)

A pattern of behavior that is so extensive that it can be described from a clinical point of view as narcissism can be noted in the four main characters. This is a trait that has already been discussed in connection with Estragon and Pozzo, in whom it is most evident, and the examples of their egocentricity cited in that discussion are applicable here. Pozzo's delusions of grandeur emanate from a narcissistic tendency. The failure of the characters to communicate is also indicative of narcissism. Each character remains absorbed in his own revery (in the case of Lucky, a virtual catatonic withdrawal), and Pozzo, Estragon, and Vladimir talk at cross-purposes much of the time, suggesting that the only real subject of interest is the self. One example of this breakdown in communication is sufficient here:

Pozzo: J'avais une très bonne vue . . . mais êtes-vous des amis?
Estragon (riant bruyamment): Il demande si nous sommes des amis!
Vladimir: Non il veut dire des amis à lui. (p. 97)

[*Pozzo:* I used to have wonderful sight—but are you friends?
Estragon: (laughing noisily). He wants to know if we are friends!
Vladimir: No, he means friends of his. (p. 54A)]

The theme of suicide running through the play can also be tied to this narcissistic strain, but that, like the problems of identity and faulty communication, overflows the narrow margins of the clinical and falls into the symbolic cluster dealing with death that is everywhere present in the play.

Obviously, any psychological analysis of literary characters must be somewhat tenuous. This is only one of many ways of viewing the play, of course; and, in the end, it merely amounts to applying specialized vocabulary to rather generalized traits. If the anomalies suggested above do not seem obvious, it is partly because Beckett is seeking generalization. It is, also, partly because Beckett has been forced, for purposes of stage presentation, to exercise greater discretion in depicting sexual aberrations than he is inclined to do in his novels. Finally, in any discussion of the apparent psychological abnormalities lurking in the sordid background of the play, it must not be forgotten that many if not all of the manifestations of the maladies just mentioned contribute in part and perhaps in the main to the grosser levels of physical comedy that accompany higher levels of comedy in the play. But the play as a play and as "play" will receive special treatment at a later point in this study.

Thus, the entire play *En attendant Godot* is constructed on a complex system of paradoxes that in the Beckettian world view seem to lie at the very basis of man's nature and to incapacitate him. His mind is at war with his body, and neither one can dominate the other, nor singly cope with life. His social nature is in conflict with his equally fundamental desire for independence and solitude; so neither alone nor in company with others can he achieve complete satisfaction. As a result of this conflict he is imprisoned both internally and by social forces. This imprisonment immobilizes him and renders him powerless. Furthermore, these social forces emanate from decaying institutions that cannot be shored up by human endeavor because man's reason as well as his physical capacities are not adequate to the task.[28] As man struggles with these problems he may develop serious psychological impediments that reflect his impotence in terms of himself and in terms of others.

But as yet we have only partially discussed Beckett's world view, for within this world view man's concept of himself also includes his relationship to the cosmos. Here again man's attempt to place himself within the universe and to develop a concept of time and space also fails because of the limitations of his reflective powers, that is, the operations of his mind in terms of the past and the future.

2

MEMORY AND IDENTITY

In *En attendant Godot,* Beckett seems to say that, on the one hand, our bodies and our minds are faulty and our human relationships leave much to be desired, while on the other hand, memory, which in principle should serve as a useful tool, is characterized by defectiveness. He seems to say that memory, by which we recognize others, upon which we base our habits and our knowledge of personal as well as cosmic history, via which we interpret the present, and upon which we construct plans for the future, is inconsistent and unreliable. Indeed, we are subject to all manner of memory lapses, and our method of measuring the time through which we travel is absurd and often irrelevant. The fallibility of memory results in a skepticism toward everything we know, be it ourselves, others, or the world around us. We are, furthermore, frequently engaged in a willful effort *not* to remember, not to remember that time is passing, that it is leading us ever towards an unknown end, of which we have mere glimmers and which we prefer, erroneous though this may be, to regard as a salvation from the tedium in which we are immersed. Rather, we are engaged in an effort not to look too clearly at the evidence, the obliviousness of death, which puts an end to this vicious and meaningless routine. At this point we are most clearly *homo ludens,* frantically devising every kind of game (Pascal's famous "divertissement") in order to make time pass. Yet, upon occasion we are caught up short and remember that while we are trying to get from one moment to the next as painlessly as possible, we are at bottom waiting to be "taken out of the game,"

waiting for someone or something whose identity, indeed whose
very existence, is no clearer than our own, no more certain than
that of those around us, to deliver us from ourselves.[1] That the
someone or something in all probability will never come constitutes
the absurdity and the irony of our existence, which is betrayed by
this malfunctioning memory, be it voluntary or involuntary. Memory, then, appears from the play to be one of our chief hindrances,
memory and its products: habit, ennui, identity, and concepts of
time and of space.

Within the play memory manifests itself in a number of ways,
and yet, no matter what the way, it is inevitably unreliable. The
characters themselves recognize (and remember!) the defective nature of memory. Pozzo and Estragon make generalized comments
about their own memory. Pozzo says that his memory is defective
(p. 45), and in Act II he seems to be contending that his memory
will never function properly, for he says that he does not remember
having met anyone yesterday and that tomorrow he will not remember having met someone today (p. 102). This statement also
contains a refusal to expend the energy necessary to remember.
Estragon, who lives in the present, is apparently untroubled by his
memory lapses; for when Vladimir asks him if it is possible that he
has already forgotten, he responds that that is the way he is and
that he either forgets immediately or never (p. 70). On the other
hand, Vladimir comments in a more general manner upon the nature of memory, saying at one point that memory plays tricks on us
(p. 60) and at another point characterizing the memory of bygone
happiness as being painful. *"Memoria praeteritorum bonorum,"* he
says and adds that that must be painful (p. 99).[2]

The many types of recall in the play include voluntary and accidental. Sometimes recall is mechanical, sometimes indirect. Also,
in many instances, forgetfulness, when combined with shaky rational processes and errors in perception, results in numerous inconsistencies in the speech and behavior of the characters, in the fusion
of time as well as of ontological states, and in mistaken or uncertain
identity.

Throughout the play cases of memory lapse revolve around the
personal history of the characters and the immediate past and result

in partial recall, imprecision, and failure to communicate. Estragon, for example, does not remember who beat him and only hazily remembers where (p. 13). He does not remember what kind of school he attended (p. 13) or that he was ever in the Vaucluse (p. 71). He has only partial recall of the meeting with Pozzo and Lucky in that he remembers only the kick and the bones (pp. 70, 76). He does not remember when he threw away his shoes, but he remembers that it was because they hurt him (p. 77). In other words, he remembers only those experiences that pertain to his affective nature, as is also evident in his recollections concerning the Bible. His concern with self leads him in Act II to forget that he has seen the tree in any state whatsoever the day before, even though he had discussed with Vladimir the possibility of hanging himself on that very tree (p. 70). Likewise, Pozzo cannot retain the name of Godot even though it has been recently mentioned (pp. 33, 42). An amusing example of memory lapse occurs when Pozzo gets the attention of the three other characters with elaborate questions as to whether everybody is present, whether everybody is looking at him and is ready, and then proceeds to forget the question he has been asked (p. 35). Furthermore, Pozzo's materialistic nature is frustrated by a special type of memory lapse—he loses the symbols of his authority and affluence (pp. 40, 47, 55). Vladimir, because he is more concerned with the past and the future, has fewer memory lapses than the other characters. Nevertheless, he demonstrates this trait when, for example, he can only vaguely remember how long he and Estragon have been together, which in theory should be an important fact concerning his personal life.

Lucky demonstrates an extreme kind of memory lapse that, properly speaking, could be called a malady of the memory. His long speech in Act I shows him unable to perform the uniquely human activity of thinking and speaking coherently. He suffers from partial aphasia, which manifests itself in his stuttering (quaquaquaqua, [p. 51]; l'Acacacacadémie d'Anthropopopométrie, [p. 52];[3] etc.) and in the repetition of phrases such as "ce qui suit qui suit qui suit" (p. 52). Even though the central concept of Lucky's speech (that man has regressed) can be isolated, this speech, which gives the effect of a broken record, is rife with fragments of thought concerning

God, science, sports, geography, academism, and perhaps alluding to the geological and cultural ages of man. By Act II, however, Lucky suffers from total aphasia.[4]

In many cases the characters recognize memory lapse in themselves and make a conscious effort to overcome this problem through voluntary memory.[5] That is, sometimes one of the characters may make a willful attempt to remember the immediate or the remote past. For example, Estragon, in a rambling conversation with Vladimir, remembers that he has asked a question, but cannot remember whether it has been answered or momentarily what the question was. However, he appears to make a concerted effort to recall the question in the following passage:

> *Vladimir:* . . . Qu'est-ce que tu voulais savoir?
> *Estragon:* Je ne me rappelle plus. (*Il mâche.*) C'est ce qui m'embête.
> (*Il regarde la carotte avec appréciation, la fait tourner en l'air du bout des doigts.*) Délicieuse, ta carotte. (*Il en suce méditativement le bout.*) Attends, ça me revient. (*Il arrache une bouchée.*)
> *Vladimir:* Alors?
> *Estragon* (*la bouche pleine, distraitement*): On n'est pas lié? (p. 23, ll. 19–28).

> [*Vladimir:* What was it you wanted to know?
> *Estragon:* I've forgotten. (*Chews.*) That's what annoys me. (*He looks at the carrot appreciatively, dangles it between finger and thumb.*) I'll never forget this carrot. (*He sucks the end of it meditatively.*) Ah yes, now I remember.
> *Vladimir:* Well?
> *Estragon:* (*his mouth full, vacuously*). We're not tied? (p. 14)]

The characters frequently have difficulty sustaining their train of thought and strive to overcome this by asking what they were saying (Pozzo, pp. 43, 47; Vladimir, p. 75) or where they were when they were interrupted (p. 48). Although this type of question could be considered rhetorical, when Pozzo asks what exactly he has been asked (p. 35) he clearly enlists his interlocutors' help; furthermore, he here reenforces this plea with a nonrhetorical question as to what he was saying, uttered in a loud voice as if insisting upon assistance. Again he calls for help from Vladimir and Estragon when he asks where he has put his pipe (p. 47). Finally, when Estragon asks Vladimir to remind him to bring a rope the next day (p. 62), he exemplifies another very common manner of seeking assistance, this time for a *potential* memory lapse. Certainly, the gravity of the intention in bringing the rope ought to obviate any memory lapse; so Estragon appears to be doing little more than flirting with the idea of suicide.

A phenomenon somewhat related to voluntary memory appears in the cases where Vladimir attempts to deal with the memory lapses of Estragon and Pozzo. In an effort to launch a discussion with Estragon about the problematical Biblical accounts of the two thieves, Vladimir asks him if he remembers or if he wants him to tell the story (p. 13). These questions and the telling of the story are, of course, intended to stimulate Estragon's memory so that the conversation may proceed. In Act II Vladimir tries to get Estragon to remember the events of the previous evening with such impatient questions as "Don't you remember?" (p. 70, l. 7; p. 75, l. 25) and "Can it be you've already forgotten?" (p. 70, l. 12). A bit later in the play, Vladimir persists with similar questioning ("Maintenant qu'est-ce que nous avons fait hier soir?" [p. 76, ll. 7–8]; "Essaie de te rappeler" [p. 76, l. 10]; "Tu ne te rappelles aucun fait, aucune circonstance?" [p. 76, ll. 17–18]; "Tu n'as rien remarqué d'insolite?" [p. 76, l. 22], etc.). However, in none of these passages do such questions have much effect upon Estragon's memory. Vladimir also meets with similar failure when he attempts to make Pozzo recall having met him and Estragon the previous evening (if, in fact, it was the previous evening) when he asks him again if he does not remember ("Vous ne vous rappelez pas?" [p. 102]). Apparently, then, memory lapse plays a considerable role in Beckett's overall portrait of memory as a defective tool.

In *En attendant Godot* numerous cases of the evocation of the past are not necessarily connected with memory lapse but do further illustrate the ineffectiveness of memory in coping with human existence. Pozzo, for example, plunges into a revery as he talks about his and Lucky's past, when nothing in the conversation is relevant to his remarks (p. 38). He must be asked twice what a "knouk" is before he can be brought out of these musings. This incident in the play is the mark of the role memory can play in an individual as self-centered as Pozzo is.

However, in some instances the conversation or events of the play do stimulate the characters' memory of the past. As Vladimir and Estragon discuss in Act I the length of time they have been together, Estragon remembers somewhat accidentally the day he threw himself into the Durance. This evokes from Vladimir the recollection that they were working at that time ("On faisait les vendanges" [p. 63]). In Act II the two men discuss the spot they find themselves in at present in relationship to where they were yesterday. When Estragon maintains that he has always been in the same spot, in the sands and the mire, Vladimir responds that the present landscape is scarcely similar to the Vaucluse ("Tout de même, tu ne vas pas me dire que ça [geste] ressemble au Vaucluse. Il y a quand même une grosse différence" [p. 71].). He is pushed by Estragon's denial that he has never been in the Vaucluse to present further evidence gathered from his memories of the past, and he insists that they have indeed been in the Vaucluse, where they worked for a man named Bonnelly ("Pourtant nous avons été ensemble dans le Vaucluse, j'en mettrais ma main au feu. Nous avons fait les vendanges, tiens, chez un nommé Bonnelly, à Roussillon" [p. 71]). The whole discussion concerning the Vaucluse is symbolic of the inconsistency and the unreliability of memory in the recollection of one's personal history.

The past sometimes is alluded to with the cliché "in the good old days," as when Estragon says "Dos à dos comme au bon vieux temps" (p. 85). Obviously, if he and Estragon were back to back, they worked as much at cross-purposes in the old days as they frequently seemed to do in the present.[6] Perhaps, then, memory softens suffering and discord.

In addition, linguistic expressions may trigger accidental and irrelevant memory, creating at times a humorous effect. Such is the case when Pozzo introduces himself and Vladimir, associating the sound of the name Pozzo with Gozzo, says that he once knew a family named Gozzo, and that the mother of that family did embroidery ("J'ai connu une famille Gozzo. La mère brodait au tambour" [p. 26]). Similarly, Estragon seems to remember twice in succession that they are waiting for Godot (pp. 101, 105), apparently as a result of formulaic language, for he has consistently forgotten this vital fact throughout the course of the play. That he does not really remember is evidenced by the fact that in a matter of moments Vladimir must again tell him that the reason they will return tomorrow is that Godot has not come and they must wait for him again (p. 108).

Another type of uncertain and somewhat mechanical recall based upon indirect evidence is discernible when Vladimir speaks of Estragon's remembering that Lucky injured him ("Ah, tu te rappelles enfin qu'il t'a fait quelque chose") to which Estragon replies that he remembers nothing, but that Vladimir has told him that that is what happened ("Je ne me rappelle rien du tout. C'est toi qui me l'as dit" [p. 100].).

Finally, at least three instances in the play illustrate inconsistencies concerning what one says or believes about one's past. Estragon recalls at one point having thrown himself into the Durance and yet at another point denies that he has ever been in the Vaucluse. Furthermore, he appears not to know who the Saviour is (p. 13),[7] yet he emulates him when he defends going barefoot by saying that Jesus did it (p. 62). The scatterbrained Pozzo also demonstrates this trait when, after twice consulting his watch (pp. 27, 43), he appears to mislay it and then decides that he has left it at the chateau (p. 56). Memory, then, in all its ramifications puts us in a position where we can know nothing for sure about ourselves or about others.[8]

This fallibility of memory, together with the ineffectiveness of reason and the senses, produces skepticism in the characters concerning knowledge based upon memory, ontological states, and identity of self as well as the identity and recognition of others. Vladimir, who *appears* to have the best memory of the four men in the play, nevertheless is led to doubt his beliefs when they are challenged by Estragon. When early in Act I Estragon wants to know if they are waiting in the right place and on the right day, Vladimir appears to waver and seeks in his pocket for the note he probably made, which would establish proof that they are in the right place and on the right day. He fails to produce this evidence, however (pp. 15, 17). Vladimir becomes even more flustered when Estragon attempts to pin him down as to which Saturday they were to come and whether this day is indeed Saturday (p. 17). In Act II a similar situation arises when Estragon confuses Vladimir about whether it is dawn or dusk. Vladimir confesses to being momentarily shaken and again seeks to shore up his belief that it is dusk by assuring Pozzo that the day is nearly over ("C'est le soir, monsieur, nous sommes arrivés au soir. Mon ami essaie de m'en faire douter, et je dois avouer que j'ai été ébranlé pendant un instant. Mais ce n'est pas pour rien que j'ai vécu cette longue journée et je peux vous assurer qu'elle est presque au bout de son répertoire" [p. 99, ll. 1–6]). As these quotations suggest, Estragon is the most skeptical of the group, a fact that is born out by Vladimir when he says that Estragon takes the cake when it comes to casting doubt on something ("ma foi . . . (se fâchant.) Pour jeter le doute, à toi le pompon" [p. 16]).[9] Clearly, these passages are intended to demonstrate the inability of even the most rational to be sure of the seemingly obvious bits of knowledge upon which activities are based.

Similar doubt and confusion arise in the characters' minds concerning states of being. They frequently have difficulty distinguishing between sleep and death and sleep and wakefulness (i.e., dream and reality); so an atmosphere of somnambulism pervades the play. In Act II Vladimir seems unable to decide whether Lucky is asleep or dead (pp. 91, 100, 102). Pozzo, on the other hand, when discussing his blindness says that one day he woke up blind and that he sometimes wonders whether he is still asleep ("Un beau jour je me suis réveillé, aveugle comme le destin. [Un temps.] Je me demande parfois si je ne dors pas encore" [p. 99]). Vladimir, musing over the sleeping Estragon, reflects this fusion of dream and reality when he says,

> Est-ce que j'ai dormi, pendant que les autres souffraient? Est-ce que je dors en ce moment? Demain, quand je croirai me réveiller, que dirai-je de cette journée? Qu'avec Estragon mon ami, à cet endroit, jusqu'à la tombée de la nuit, j'ai attendu Godot? Que Pozzo est passé, avec son porteur, et qu'il nous a parlé? Sans doute. Mais dans tout cela qu'y aura-t-il de vrai? . . . Lui ne saura rien. Il parlera des coups qu'il a reçus et je lui donnerai une carotte. . . . A cheval sur une tombe et une naissance difficile. Du fond du trou, rêveusement, le fossoyeur applique ses fers. . . . Moi aussi, un autre me regarde, en se disant, Il dort, il ne sait pas; qu'il dorme (pp. 105–06).

[*Vladimir:* Was I sleeping, while the others suffered? Am I sleeping now? To-morrow, when I wake, or think I do, what shall I say of to-day? That with Estragon my friend, at this place until the fall of night, I waited for Godot? That Pozzo passed, with his carrier, and that he spoke to us? Probably. But in all that what truth will there be? . . . He'll know nothing. He'll tell me about the blows he received and I'll give him a carrot. . . Astride of a grave and a difficult birth. Down in the hole, lingeringly, the grave-digger puts on the forceps. . . . At me too someone is looking, of me too someone is saying, He is sleeping, he knows nothing, let him sleep on. (pp. 58–58A)]

As is evident in the preceding passage, as well as in Pozzo's remark that one day we are born and that one day we die, on the same day, in fact ("Un jour nous sommes nés, un jour nous mourrons, le même jour. . . . "[p. 104]), states of birth and death are also fused in the play. These fusions of states of being, which would probably not occur even granting our faulty memory if only our reason and our senses were more discerning, provide additional illustrations of the skepticism that is everywhere present in our lives, although it is not always recognized as such.

It can be concluded from the play, however, that fusions of states of being, though problematical, do not offer such an extreme form of skepticism as is manifested in the inability to fix the identity of self or of others. Identity, which grows out of memory combined with knowledge or belief, is generally associated first of all with name, then with date of birth (age), place of birth, residence, profession, and possessions. All of these fallacious marks of identity are utilized without success by us as well as by the various characters, some leaning more heavily on one mark, some on another.

Name, though usually accepted as a significant mark of identity, cannot be used as an index to the identity of the characters in *En attendant Godot*. The two main characters have several names, depending upon the perspective from which they are viewed. In the context of their friendship, the affectionate nicknames Didi and Gogo appear,[10] whereas when Pozzo asks Estragon his name he rapidly responds, "Catulle" (p. 43). On the other hand, the messenger boy mysteriously addresses Vladimir as "Monsieur Albert"

(p. 58). What is most unusual is that the name Vladimir appears only once in the dialogue of the play, and Estragon never. As a result of this, Vladimir and Estragon are Vladimir and Estragon only to the reader, not to the playgoing audience. An additional puzzle concerning names arises in the second act when Vladimir refers to Pozzo's slave as Lucky, but the name Lucky (suggestive of the name of a dog or other animal—a beast of burden, perhaps) never appeared in the dialogue of Act I.[11] Furthermore, while the theme of the play centers around waiting for Godot, it is not certain that this is indeed his name, as is demonstrated by the exchange between Vladimir and Estragon in which Estragon asks if his name is Godot ("Il s'appelle Godot?") to which Vladimir answers that he thinks so ("Je crois" [p. 24].).[12] Pozzo is the only character who asserts his identity by saying repeatedly that his name is Pozzo (twice on page 25), and yet in Act II he fails to respond to this name; so Estragon is moved to propose that they try others (p. 96), as if to suggest that his identity is not linked to the name Pozzo. This indeed seems to be the case, for he appears to respond to the name Abel and a bit later to the name Cain (p. 96).[13]

This ambiguity in the names of the characters makes their identity one of the principal difficulties of the play from the audience's point of view. It implies that the characters may have more than one identity, in keeping with Beckett's concept of the individual as set forth in his essay *Proust*, in which he writes, "Or rather life is a succession of habits, since the individual is a succession of individuals. . . ."[14] Although it is a mistake to believe that one can be identified by one's name alone, it is even more difficult to establish identity if one's name is not clear. Thus, as is generally recognized, knowledge about one's self or others derived from names is highly undependable (and extremely unsatisfactory).

The epithets employed by the characters in the play sometimes obscure and sometimes clarify their identity and their relationships. The friendship between Vladimir and Estragon, for example, is spelled out when Vladimir, handing Estragon a carrot, says, "Voilà, mon cher" (p. 23), and in the English version when he calls him "dear fellow" (p. 14A).[15] However, Pozzo's relationship to Estragon and Vladimir is blurred by the direct and indirect epithets he uses when referring to them. At various points he refers to them as his "friends" (pp. 27, 28), as his "peers" (p. 28), his "good people" (p. 45), and he calls Estragon his "good fellow" (p. 30). These clichés may well be indicative of insincerity, a notion supported by his allusions to Estragon and Vladimir as strangers or foreigners (pp. 25, 37). These appellations are in sharp contrast to those he applies to Lucky throughout the play. Repeatedly he addresses Lucky as a pig, a dungheap, and the like ("porc," "pouacre," and "charogne" [pp. 16, 27, 31, 46, 51, 54, 57, 103, etc.]); so he is greatly amused at the application of the title "Monsieur" to Lucky (p. 31). Vladimir falls into the same disrespectful pattern as Pozzo when he calls Estragon a pig (p. 79), and both Vladimir and Estragon, imitating Pozzo and Lucky a bit later in the play, call each other ugly names ("salaud," "fumier," "crapule" and "cochon," as well as "porc" [p. 84]). Respect is granted Vladimir when the messenger boy addresses him as "Monsieur Albert" and "Monsieur," despite the fact that Vladimir quite obviously does not occupy the social station in keeping with this title (pp. 59–60, 106–07). Interestingly, in both of Vladimir's conversations with the boy, Godot is referred to not simply as "Godot" but as "Monsieur Godot," thus placing Vladimir more or less on the same social level as Godot. Again, these epithets may be mere clichés, or they may be an indication of a relationship. In either case, the identity of a character cannot be established from them because frequently they are contradicted by other indications of the social condition of the person.

The identity of the characters, furthermore, cannot be established by means of such conventional marks as age, place of birth and residence, profession, or possessions. Although indications in the play suggest that these men are beyond their prime, just how old they are never becomes clear, to each other or to us. Pozzo claims to be older than Lucky, despite appearances (p. 38), and the only evidence that sheds any light on the matter is Pozzo's statement that he and Lucky have been together for nearly sixty years (p. 38). Vladimir, on the other hand, never responds to Pozzo's direct question as to how old he is ("Quel âge avez-vous, sans indiscrétion?" [p. 32]), and he is also indefinite about the number of years that he and Estragon have been together: he thinks it has been fifty years, *maybe* ("Je ne sais pas. Cinquante ans peut-être" [p. 63].). This vagueness on the part of Pozzo and Vladimir makes it impossible to establish their identity on the basis of their pasts.

Place of origin and habitation of the characters, which ordinarily would also be marks of identity, are no easier to establish than are their names and ages. Pozzo, the only character to provide any clues to his origin, declares that it is divine (p. 38)! In addition, he provides only scattered bits of information about his habitation and social position. One knows that he owns the land along the road upon which Vladimir and Estragon are waiting (p. 27), that he apparently resides in a chateau (p. 56), and that he owns slaves and many other possessions. And yet, knowing all these things, one does not really know who Pozzo is. The identities of Estragon and Vladimir cannot be clearly established either; even though in Act I Estragon says to Pozzo that they are not of the region ("Nous ne sommes pas d'ici, Monsieur" [p. 26]), in Act II he insists that he has never been anywhere else (p. 71, 1. 10). This ambiguity obviates the possibility of establishing their origins or their present place of residence. Despite this ambiguity, much in the play indicates that Estragon and Vladimir have no place of residence and no possessions.

Profession, another conventional sign of identity, is similarly inapplicable because one simply cannot establish the profession of any of the characters. At different points in the play one is led to believe that Pozzo is perhaps a landowner, or a priest, or a politician, etc., but at no point is one permitted to choose any one profession over the others. As for Lucky's profession, Pozzo notes that it is not, or that it was not previously, that of porter (pp. 30, 36); what his profession is, or was, is not clear, despite the fact that one knows that the roles of Pozzo and Lucky might have been reversed (p. 36), a fact that tells one very little.[16] Estragon maintains that he was once a poet (p. 13), but it must be concluded from their present circumstances that although they work at some "turbot" after which they meet neither Vladimir nor Estragon currently has any characterizing profession.

What Beckett seems to be saying, then, is that we are unable to establish a person's identity by traditional means (name, age, place, profession, and possessions). He may even intend to imply that identity cannot be established at all.[17]

Thus, the identity of the four characters cannot be discovered by looking at their social profile, nor do they seem to have any true identity as individuals.[18] What does seem clear is that they are all members of the human race. Pozzo recognizes this identifying feature in Vladimir and Estragon as well as in himself when he calls them human beings and says that they are of the same species as he ("Vous êtes bien des êtres humains cependant. . . . A ce que je vois. . . . De la même espèce que moi. . . ." [p. 26].). And even though Pozzo does not appear to consider Lucky a human being Vladimir criticizes Pozzo's inhuman treatment of Lucky, thus revealing that he, for one, considers Lucky to be human ("Traiter un homme de cette façon . . . je trouve ça . . . un être humain . . . non . . . c'est une honte!" [p. 32].). Vladimir, replying to Pozzo's question as to who he is, does not give proper names, as would be expected, but instead simply says that they are men (p. 94). This response is a follow-up to his previous statement that he and Estragon represent all of mankind, whether they like it or not (p. 91). What emerges from all of this is a generalized portrait of the human race, half of which wanders aimlessly, no matter what objectives it may delude itself with having, the other half of which spends its time waiting for something, perhaps in the form of a person whose identity is very hazy, someone or something to deliver mankind from an almost unbearable ennui.

It is in Godot, who never appears in the play and yet is a pivotal character,[19] that Vladimir's hope for salvation lies. (Estragon is not concerned with salvation; he simply follows the routine set up by Vladimir.) We wonder, with Pozzo, who Godot is (p. 26). Vladimir and Estragon regard him as a man of means, and he appears to be the hub in a social circle—he has friends, agents, etc. With such attributes, he is no doubt powerful (p. 21). Vladimir contends that Godot, a father figure like himself, is a source of creature comforts (p. 22).[20] However, the signs of benevolence implicit in these creature comforts are belied by the messenger boy's admission that Godot beats his brother (p. 60). Apparently, some connection exists between these beatings and the fact that Godot owns sheep and goats, the former of which are tended by the brother. In other words (if this reference to sheep and goats is construed as a Biblical allusion) Godot has province over all peoples; this, along with the fact that Vladimir and Estragon admit to having prayed to Godot (p. 20), gives Godot godlike characteristics. This may also be indicated by the boy's hesitant affirmation that Godot, like Nobodaddy, has a long white beard (p. 107). This thesis is further supported not only by the suggestiveness of his name, but also by the belief Vladimir holds that Godot, like a *deus ex machina*, will arrive to save them (pp. 84, 109), as well as by the fear Vladimir has that Godot will punish them if they drop him (p. 108). Yet nothing in all of this evidence forces the conclusion that Godot is God. He could be no more than an extremely powerful person. But he could also be a symbol, a symbol of man's futile hope, which constitutes a motivation, feeble though it may be, for "continuing," and this seems to be far more likely. Thus, the identity of Godot can no more be ascertained than can that of the other four characters.

Perhaps it could be argued that the presence of the messenger boy establishes the existence of Godot as a certainty. It also could be argued that if Godot is God, the messenger boy is his angel; whereas if Godot is merely a wealthy and powerful man, then the messenger and his brother are Godot's servants and errand boys. However, if Godot is a floating symbol for man's hope (false or otherwise), then the messenger boy is whatever comes man's way to shore up this hope. Thus, it is possible to deny not only the existence of Godot but even that of the messenger boy despite the latter's appearance in the play, for the boy could be construed as a figment of the imagination.

When identity is uncertain, the ability to remember and to recognize others is affected. Therefore, mistaken identity and failure to recognize places and persons occur throughout the play in abundance. Estragon, for instance, fails to recognize the place where he and Vladimir find themselves in Act II (p. 70) as being the same place in which they had waited for Godot the very day before.[21] Since in Act I he has ostensibly never seen Godot, it is perhaps too surprising that he mistakes Pozzo for him (even though he has supposedly become acquainted with Pozzo the very day before [p. 88]). Strangely, after Pozzo's disappearance in Act II Estragon wonders if Pozzo might not have been Godot and designates both Pozzo and Godot by name (p. 105). This confusion on the part of Estragon has been cited by some critics as evidence for the theory that Pozzo and Godot are one.[22] It is more probable that Estragon's faulty memory and scant information regarding both Pozzo and Godot are at the source of this mistaken identity. In fact, the very presence in *En attendant Godot* of the *qui pro quo*, although it is a traditional device of comedy, supports the view that for Beckett man is enmeshed in a skepticism that hinders his identifying himself, others, or the world.

Estragon is not the only character who fails to recognize others. In Acts I and II (pp. 60, 106), Vladimir and the messenger boy exchange questions and answers indicating that neither is sure he has seen the other before. So intense is the recognition problem in this case that it casts doubt on whether it is the same boy who appears on both occasions. If Vladimir and Estragon were to find themselves face to face with Godot, they would probably not recognize him, since they both confess to Pozzo that they barely know him (p. 26). Moreover, Pozzo fails to recognize Vladimir and Estragon in the second act (pp. 94, 102), a failure due in part to his blindness but also attributable to his faulty memory and to his egocentric personality, which has not allowed him to formulate a clear idea of the identity of either Vladimir or Estragon (if indeed either has one). Finally, of utmost significance is Vladimir's statement to Estragon that they do know Pozzo and Lucky, that they have seen them before (p. 58). This could mean that Pozzo and Lucky are *types* whom Estragon and Vladimir have met before; that is, he may be confusing types and particular individuals. Then again, Vladimir does know Lucky's name, and since the characters in the play constantly manifest contradictions and inconsistencies in their thought it is possible that Vladimir and Estragon have indeed seen these very men before. What is most troublesome in this passage is Vladimir's statement that no one ever recognizes *them,* an assertion he makes in refutation of Estragon's claim that they do not know Pozzo and Lucky because Pozzo and Lucky did not recognize them. Vladimir's statement lends itself to several interpretations. He may mean that since people seek the identity of a person through external signs they never arrive at his true identity, the essential self. The question of course arises whether Beckett believes there is such an essential self or whether, on the contrary, he believes that each person is a series of individuals, that one's identity is floating—a state of being that makes recognition difficult if not impossible. This would explain why Vladimir says that no one ever recognizes them.

By no means is it accidental, however, that Vladimir and Estragon recognize each other. Although the readers, the audience, the outsiders cannot arrive at the essential identity of Vladimir and Estragon—just as they themselves cannot identify other characters in the play—certain stable factors of recognition and habit make Didi always known to Gogo and Gogo always known to Didi.[23] Perhaps one of the reasons for this is that the mind knows its body and the body its mind. But insofar as these two domains conflict, the separate identity of the domains, as well as of the two characters, is asserted. At this point the truth of Sypher's remark concerning Beckett's characters is evident: "We cannot, in spite of everything, annihilate selfhood."[24] Thus, the self always knows the self and cannot escape the self even though others may not recognize its essence and even though one is, by another set of criteria, a series of individuals. Hence, the problem of identity in this play is linked with solipsism, which plays a dominant role in Beckett's world view.

Still another and final explanation for Vladimir's complaint that no one ever recognizes them may be that he is voicing here the frustration a writer experiences at not having his clues properly interpreted. If so, then Vladimir and Estragon are symbols that the reader or the audience fails to decipher. If Vladimir and Estragon are indeed metaphors for a large section of humanity absurdly waiting for a never-to-be-realized salvation, then Vladimir's remark means that humanity as represented by them fails to recognize itself in them and therefore to assess its true condition.

This condition, as the play clearly demonstrates, is governed largely by a fallacious memory that makes personal identity uncertain and recognition difficult if not impossible.

3

ASPECTS OF TIME AND PLACE

In addition to the role memory plays in dealing with identity and recognition, it also gives rise to our notions of past, present, and future, as well as to our conceptualization of place. These notions, as they are related to life, involve extensive absurdity, in Beckett's view. The picture that emerges from the play is that our knowledge of the past (our sense of history) is based upon unreliable memory; our experience of the present is filled with boredom and the need to cope with this boredom; and our anticipation of the future rests upon a poorly grounded hope of salvation. In short, the skepticism that man's memory produces in other contexts can also be detected in the relationship it has to temporal and spatial matters.

The ridiculousness of such temporal and spatial orientations is depicted in *En attendant Godot* not only through the characters' difficulty in coping with problems of past, present, and future but also in their efforts to measure time, as well as to locate themselves geographically. Such absurdities are further underlined by the vagueness of the time and locus of the play itself, not to mention the most salient factor of all—the radical physical changes in Pozzo and Lucky, and in the natural surroundings, which appear to occur overnight. The characters of the play taken as a whole probably represent universal man. Similarly, the indefiniteness of time and place indicates that man's predicament is not dependent upon a particular time or place but upon his need to deal with the known or unknown past, the ennui of his present, and the expectations he associates with the future. And this can be said of man in general, whether or not the individual man conceives of time in this tripartite manner.

The unique problems involved in these elements of time appear in various guises in *En attendant Godot*. The inadequacy of the characters in dealing with their own pasts has been noted already; their incompetence with respect to historical problems is equally great. This particular concern with the past, of course, may be one of the many games devised by them to dispose of the eternal present, in which the specters of habit, the inability to change, inertia, and ennui constantly appear.[1] While Vladimir and Estragon achieve a certain amount of relief from this ennui by inventing games to make time pass, permanent relief for Vladimir resides only in his hope that Godot will arrive to save them. Thus, while Estragon is a creature of the moment, Vladimir consistently views the present in terms of the future.

It is Vladimir, also, who raises a historical question concerning the validity of St. Luke the Evangelist's account of the two thieves, which is the only account in the Gospels in which one of the thieves is saved. He pursues this problem by pointing out to Estragon that by Saint Matthew's account both thieves reviled Christ, while the story of the two thieves does not even appear in the other two Gospels. The essence of the "problem" is that Saint Luke's account is the only version that everyone believes or knows. Vladimir's skepticism, which becomes our own, is double-edged. He is pointing out, on the one hand, that no evidence exists for accepting one historian's account over another; he is implying, on the other hand, that the Gospels, if they contradict one another, cannot be divinely inspired.[2] Vladimir's preoccupation with the story of the two thieves, coming as it does in the early movement of *En attendant Godot*, introduces the continuing theme of salvation present in the play. But Vladimir also is expressing a profound reason for doubting that salvation will ever come about, even though (or perhaps because) salvation is his major preoccupation. Estragon, on the other hand, concerns himself with neither the historical nor the theological portents of this problem, since his security and salvation rest predominantly in Vladimir. That Estragon is indeed far from being a historian is shown both in his attitude towards the historical past (the history of the race) and in his disregard for his personal history. Yet his primary interest, which is the present, is not his alone: Vladimir, albeit for different reasons, shares Estragon's involvement in the present.

The existence of these two men is habit ridden, and their reigning habit among habits is their friendship; that is, they are held together as much by habit as by any need. They frequently speak of separating, even in the final scene, yet they always reunite at the end of the day to wait for Godot, and the suggestion at the end of the play is that this will always be the case. The following bit of dialogue on page 71, in which Estragon suggests that they would be better off apart and Vladimir replies that Estragon always says this and yet always comes back, corroborates this theory:

> *Estragon:* On ferait mieux de se séparer.
> *Vladimir:* Tu dis toujours ça. Et chaque fois tu reviens.

Apparently their greatest need for one another is to help each other pass time and to alleviate each other's boredom, thus giving to each other the impression of existing (p. 79).

If their friendship is habitual, so too are their activities when together, such as the invention of games and routine conversations meant to kill time while waiting for Godot, which in its turn is another habit (p. 44). The security of habit makes change extremely difficult, of course, and this is recognized by Estragon and Vladimir, first in one of their vaudeville routines toward the beginning of the play:

> *Estragon:* On a beau se démener.
> *Vladimir:* On reste ce qu'on est.
> *Estragon:* On a beau se tortiller.
> *Vladimir:* Le fond ne change pas.
> *Estragon:* Rien à faire. (p. 24)

> [*Estragon:* No use struggling.
> *Vladimir:* One is what one is.
> *Estragon:* No use wiggling.
> *Vladimir:* The essential doesn't change.
> *Estragon:* Nothing to be done. (p. 14A)]

and later when Estragon and Vladimir discuss the change that supposedly has taken place in Pozzo and Lucky:

> *Vladimir:* Ils ont beaucoup changé.
> *Estragon:* Qui?
> *Vladimir:* Ces deux-là.
> *Estragon:* C'est ça, faisons un peu de conversation.
> *Vladimir:* N'est-ce pas qu'ils ont beaucoup changé?
> *Estragon:* C'est probable. Il n'y a que nous qui n'y arrivons pas. (p. 57)

> [*Vladimir:* How they've changed!
> *Estragon:* Who?
> *Vladimir:* Those two.
> *Estragon:* That's the idea, let's make a little conversation.
> *Vladimir:* Haven't they?
> *Estragon:* What?
> *Vladimir:* Changed.
> *Estragon:* Very likely. They all change. Only we can't. (p. 32)]

Habit, however, can be broken when the person is desperate for companionship, as when Pozzo lingers to smoke a second pipeful of tobacco, though he says this is not one of his habits (p. 32). Habit makes change difficult in part because it makes one less conscious of ennui as well as of all the more painful aspects of life and death, for habit can be a great deadener (p. 106). Vladimir is Beckett's spokesman in this instance, because in *Proust* Beckett himself advances the theory that boredom nourishes habit,[3] and that habit ". . . paralyzes our attention, drugs those handmaidens of perception whose co-operation is not absolutely essential."[4] Boredom, which in *Proust* Beckett views as "the most durable of human evils,"[5] is an *En attendant Godot* the condition that Vladimir and Estragon most wish to avoid. The play opens with the line "rien à faire" (nothing to be done), which recurs periodically though not frequently throughout the play (pp. 9, 24, 28, 78, 82 ["Que faire, que faire?"], 85). This line is open to several interpretations, one of which is that nothing can be done about the situation at hand, (i.e., removing the shoes), or else about ending the boredom, or— essentially the same thing—there is nothing to do (to pass the time, to endure the boredom). This boredom is extremely intense and is repeatedly recognized as such by Vladimir and Estragon, who make conscious efforts to overcome it. Upon recognizing their boredom, Pozzo proposes that Lucky entertain them, to make the time seem shorter (p. 45 ff.). But Vladimir and Estragon verbalize their anguish over their ennui themselves. This is apparent not only in the line "nothing to be done" but in such lines as "will night never come?" (pp. 38, 41), as well as in Estragon's more overt outcry that nothing ever happens and no one ever comes (p. 50). In a key passage toward the end of the play (p. 105), Vladimir expresses the painful tedium of their existence, filled with trivial routine activities that he realizes will never change. He says,

Demain, quand je croirai me réveiller, que dirai-je de cette journée? Qu'avec Estragon mon ami, à cet endroit, jusque'à la tombée de la nuit, j'ai attendu Godot? Que Pozzo est passé, avec son porteur, et qu'il nous a parlé? Sans doute. Mais dans tout cela qu'y aura-t-il de vrai? (*Estragon, s'étant acharné en vain sur ses chaussures, s'est assoupi à nouveau. Vladimir le regarde.*) Lui ne saura rien. Il parlera des coups qu'il a reçus et je lui donnerai une carotte.

[To-morrow, when I wake, or think I do, what shall I say of today? That with Estragon my friend, at this place, until the fall of night, I waited for Godot? That Pozzo passed, with his carrier, and that he spoke to us? Probably. But in all that what truth will there be? (*Estragon, having struggled with his boots in vain, is dozing off again. Vladimir looks at him.*) He'll know nothing. He'll tell me about the blows he received and I'll give him a carrot. (p. 58)]

Vladimir feels momentarily that he cannot continue with this meaningless routine, but then, as if he has surprised and shocked himself, he wonders what he can have said (p. 106). Vladimir and Estragon contemplate several possible courses of action for getting out of their rut, the two most important being a departure from the scene and suicide. But they do not leave the scene of the supposed rendezvous because they are unable to do so—they remain inert.[6] And they do not commit suicide because they are, again, unable to do so—they do not have the proper tools, and in all probability they are not thoroughly convinced that they want to die.[7] When all is said and done, tedium, it seems, is preferable to death.[8]

Instead, the main way in which Vladimir and Estragon confront their ennui is with the invention of a succession of various games designed to make time pass imperceptibly "while waiting for Godot." But the invention of games and other diversions is not only a means of killing time, it is also a means by which the characters give themselves the impression of existing (p. 79).[9] The games that they invent are conspicuously theatrical in nature. They range from the simple mime (the hat game, pp. 82–83, and calisthenics, p. 87) to the more complex levels of linguistic games (throughout the play)[10] and telling each other stories (pp. 13, 18), to actual episodes of play-acting (fighting and making up [p. 86] and playing at being Pozzo and Lucky [pp. 83–84]).

Closely related to the playing of games is the utilization of other physical and mental activities to fill time. Estragon, the hedonist, eats (p. 78), sleeps (p. 80),[11] and dreams. Dreaming, as Vladimir points out (p. 104), is a way of passing time. Another form of diversion involving Estragon's physical orientation is proposed by Vladimir when he suggests that Estragon try on the "new" shoes (p. 79). When games per se give out, the two men fall back upon the mere rudiments of conversation in an effort to avoid thinking and hearing (pp. 72, 75). The important thing for them is not the content of the conversation but simply that there be conversation:

> *Vladimir:* Dis quelque chose!
> *Estragon:* Je cherche. . . .
> *Vladimir (angoissé):* Dis n'importe quoi! (p. 73)

> [*Vladimir:* Say something!
> *Estragon:* I'm trying. . . .
> *Vladimir: (in anguish).* Say anything at all! (pp. 40A–41)]

Indeed, the whole episode in Act II in which Vladimir urges Estragon to remember things about his remote and immediate past is another example of this use of conversion as a diversion (pp. 71–76). Of course, virtually all conversation between Vladimir and Estragon arises out of their desire to pass the time. Even when they are confronted with the problem of trying to gain Pozzo's attention, Estragon proposes that they try out other names on him as a means

of passing time and of perhaps falling eventually on the right name
(p. 96). Pozzo not only offers himself and Lucky as a pastime, he
succeeds in his efforts. Vladimir remarks that "that" has made time
pass (p. 57); Estragon, however, replies that it would have passed
without "that" (p. 57). In Act II Pozzo and Lucky again come to the
rescue just as Vladimir and Estragon are running out of material
(p. 88). Finally, the three passages in which the two contemplate
suicide represent a desperate means of disposing of time, although
this would not be the exclusive interpretation of the three passages
(pp. 18, 62, 108).

While these games and the other diversions are primarily undertaken to while away the time and to confirm existence, they are
also a way, an unsuccessful way, of trying to escape the oppres-
siveness of silence and the feeling of solitude that tend to engulf the
individual. Although the characters are rarely alone on stage, at the
beginning of Act I Estragon is busily engaged in trying to take off
his shoes, and at the beginning of Act II Vladimir is entertaining
himself by singing a round. However, the vast majority of these
games and modes of entertainment involve two or more of the characters. This concept of togetherness is expressed by Estragon when
he asks Vladimir if he does not think that they get along pretty well
together (p. 79). The notion that self-expression should not be undertaken independently can be detected in Estragon's resentment
upon finding Vladimir singing to himself, as if untroubled by Estragon's absence (p. 68). But the effort to engage in any meaningful
activity with another (*autrui*) is doomed, owing to the egocentricity
of the characters, their inability to communicate, the merely habitual nature of the relationship that is based a great deal more on
psychological dependency than on fruitful fraternity. For Beckett,
such a thing as productive friendship is unrealizable or, more precisely, nonexistent.[12] Man's fundamental condition is, rather, one
of solitude, a condition that the characters in the play wish to elim-
inate. It is impossible for them to do this, but if it *were* possible and
if they *were* to succeed in doing it, then they would destroy their
individuality and all that individuality implies. Throughout the play
Beckett appears to be saying, then, that man paradoxically seeks his
identity and seeks to escape his identity in society. Man also seeks
to divert himself through society and therefore to avoid considering

the grim realities of solitude, death, and the need to atone for having been born. Through this quest, man shows himself to be far
more *Homo ludens* than *Homo sapiens.*

As *Homo ludens,* then, man plays his games to dispose of a present that is charged with ennui and in anticipation of a future that
he hopes will dissipate this ennui. Hope is the element that drives
man onward, but in *Godot,* as Jacobsen and Mueller have pointed
out, the devices of hope are hellish.[13] Jacobsen and Mueller cite
the transformation of the tree and the finding of the shoes as symbols of hope, but other things also might be construed as signs of
hope. Leaving aside the most obvious of these, the anticipation of
Godot's arrival, at least three other sources of hope may be identified—Vladimir's statement that Estragon should keep the shoes
even though they are too big for him in case he should some day
have some socks (p. 80), the episodes in which Estragon hopes to
get money from Pozzo (pp. 33, 92), and the longing for the night.
The foregoing signify varying levels of hope, ranging from the physical on up to the most spiritual.

The longing for the night expresses the desire that the ennui, the
need to pass the time, and the waiting may come to an end. With
the night comes sleep, a state much like death, and with sleep or
death there is oblivion. Such oblivion is the only acceptable alternative to waiting for Godot (p. 91), suicide being an impossibility.
Vladimir expresses this desire for the night when he asks if the night
will never come (pp. 38, 41). The symbolic significance of the night
(representative of death and oblivion) is revealed when Pozzo says,
". . . mais derrière ce voile de douceur et de calme . . . la nuit
galope . . . et viendra se jeter sur nous . . . pfft! comme ça . . . au
moment où nous nous y attendrons le moins" (p. 44) [". . . but behind this veil of gentleness and peace night is charging . . . and will
burst upon us . . . pop! like that! . . . just when we least expect it"
(p. 25A)]. Clearly there are only two possibilities, judging from
Vladimir's statement: they are waiting for Godot or else for nightfall
(p. 91).

But the alternative offered by the night (unless it means death)
is merely a temporary relief from the tribulations of existence. Godot, on the other hand, represents permanent salvation from the
anguish of ennui (pp. 84, 109). The theme of salvation is introduced

by Vladimir's discussion of the two thieves and carried along by mention of the Saviour (p. 13), reenforced by an allusion to Jesus (p. 52), and to Cain and Abel (p. 96).[14] These allusions, which (along with the presence of the tree) have led some to see *En attendant Godot* as a theologically oriented play, are more likely ornamentations accompanying the major salvation motif, which is Godot. But since, contrary to Bentley,[15] we believe that there is reason to hold that Godot will never come, we contend that the meaning of the play is that, although man continues to hope for his salvation (in other words, his deliverance from his predicament), he does so in vain.[16] In fact, Vladimir demonstrates that he does not really believe that Godot will come when he asks the messenger boy if he is sure that he has seen him or if he is going to come tomorrow and say that he has never seen him ("Dis, tu es bien sûr de m'avoir vu, tu ne vas pas me dire demain que tu ne m'as jamais vu?" [p. 107]), which shows that he expects the messenger boy and not Godot tomorrow. In addition, three carefully distributed passages in *En attendant Godot* clearly suggest that the future for Vladimir and Estragon holds nothing essentially different from their present or their past.[17] The following quotations, one of which has already been cited in another context (see p. 105 of the play; English, p. 58), serve to demonstrate this thesis:

(one)
Vladimir: Il n'a pas dit ferme qu'il viendrait.
Estragon: Et s'il ne vient pas?
Vladimir: Nous reviendrons demain.
Estragon: Et puis après-demain.
Vladimir: Peut-être.
Estragon: Et ainsi de suite.
Vladimir: C'est-à-dire . . .
Estragon: Jusqu'à ce qu'il vienne.
Vladimir: Tu es impitoyable.
Estragon: Nous sommes déjà venus hier. (p. 16)

[*Vladimir:* He didn't say for sure he'd come.
Estragon: And if he doesn't come?
Vladimir: We'll come back to-morrow.
Estragon: And then the day after to-morrow.
Vladimir: Possibly.

Estragon: And so on.
Vladimir: The point is—
Estragon: Until he comes.
Vladimir: You're merciless.
Estragon: We came here yesterday. (pp. 10–10A)]

(two)
Vladimir: J'ai froid.
Estragon: On est venu trop tôt.
Vladimir: C'est toujours à la tombée de la nuit.
Estragon: Mais la nuit ne tombe pas.
Vladimir: Elle tombera tout d'un coup, comme hier.
Estragon: Puis ce sera la nuit.
Vladimir: Et nous pourrons partir.
Estragon: Puis ce sera encore le jour. . . . Que faire, que faire? (p. 82)

[*Vladimir:* I'm cold.
Estragon: We came too soon.
Vladimir: It's always at nightfall.
Estragon: But night doesn't fall.
Vladimir: It'll fall all of a sudden, like yesterday.
Estragon: Then it'll be night.
Vladimir: And we can go.
Estragon: Then it'll be day again. (*Pause. Despairing.*) What'll we do, what'll we do! (pp. 45A–46)]

The absurdity of man's temporal orientation within this humdrum existence is reflected not only in the characters' attitudes toward time but also in their futile attempts at measuring its passage.[18] The irrelevance of measuring time can be observed best in Pozzo's actions and words. He prides himself on possessing a watch that has a high degree of accuracy ("une véritable savonnette. Messieurs, à secondes trotteuses" [p. 55].), and he consults this watch in order to give his words an unnecessary degree of precision. ("Voyez-vous, la route est longue quand on chemine tout seul pendant . . . [*il regarde sa montre*] . . . pendant . . . [*il calcule*] . . . Six heures, oui, c'est bien ça, six heures à la file . . ." [p. 27]. Compare: "Il y a une heure [*il regarde sa montre, ton prosaïque*] environ . . ." [p. 43].). His obsession with time leads him to express great anxiety when Vladimir claims that time has stopped. He would rather believe anything than this, and, putting his watch to his ear, he urges Vladimir to believe anything but that (p. 42). Pozzo recognizes that when time stops, death ensues, but he estimates the validity of Vladimir's remark in terms of his watch and not in terms of life. This confusion between the man-made mechanism for measuring time and a natural instrument for marking it occurs again, this time in reverse, when Estragon mistakes the sound of Pozzo's heartbeat for the ticking of his watch (p. 55). Pozzo also shows his concern with time in his need to be punctual, though the ends of this punctuality are not divulged ("Mais il est temps que je vous quitte, si je ne veux pas me mettre en retard" [p. 42]). Pozzo's precision is in contrast with Vladimir's imprecision in accounting for the passage of time. While Pozzo seeks to be absolutely exact in telling how long he and Lucky have been together ("Il y aura bientôt soixante ans que ça dure . . . [il calcule mentalement] . . . oui, bientôt soixante" [p. 38]), Vladimir remains vague concerning how long he and Estragon have been together when he says that it has been about fifty years (p. 10), but too much time has gone by; he adds that it is too late now (p. 11). This vagueness concerning time also occurs at intervals in Lucky's speech, which is interspersed with such clichés as, "ça viendra," "on a le temps" ("that will come," "there's enough time"). These expressions, which show a type of optimism, are ironically inconsistent with the general theme of Lucky's speech, man's physical and cultural regression.

Radical changes occur overnight in the play and thus reflect the absurdity of the character's attitudes toward temporal matters. These changes take place in nature (symbolized by the tree) and in Pozzo and Lucky (i.e., the former's blindness and the latter's muteness). The changes have come about because they are in no way connected to habit or the human will; they are of a purely physical nature. Furthermore, the change in the tree suggests that nature partakes of a fruitful cycle in which human beings do not participate. Quite the contrary, where there is a renaissance in nature, there is sterility and degradation in man. The presence of these radical changes, occurring as they do in such a brief span of time, may have multiple purposes. Beckett may intend to mock man's concept of time, or he may intend to say that existence is so humdrum that all conception of time is lost; so in reality more than one day may have gone by between the two acts, though the stage directions indicate otherwise.

The triviality and absurdity of taking time seriously is further re-flected in the obscurity of the play's situation in terms of the cen-tury, the season of the year, and the time of the day. That they should have thought of suicide an eternity ago, in about 1900 (p. 10), indicates that the play takes place at some time during the 20th century, but it is in no way tied to any historical event, political or social. In fact, Vladimir and Estragon are so removed from the con-text of their era that Pozzo asks in exasperation if they even belong to the century (p. 39). That they have been together about fifty years also suggests that it is midcentury, but, since the characters them-selves are vague concerning these matters, the audience cannot be certain either. The flowering of the tree suggests that the play be-gins in late winter and ends in early spring, but the change in the tree is so sudden that it makes any fixing of the seasons precarious. Finally, despite the fact that stage directions for both acts indicate the time of day as evening (Act I, "soir"; Act II, "même heure"), the crepuscular atmosphere that pervades both acts and the fact that the characters themselves recognize that it could be either dawn or dusk (pp. 43, 98) communicate to the audience a certain ambiguity concerning the time of day. This factor, however, is alleviated by remarks and questions scattered throughout the play, such as "it's still daylight" (pp. 22, 33); "it's getting late" (p. 49); "why are you so late?" (pp. 58, 59); "Do you know what time it is?" (p. 59); "at night fall" (p. 82); "night is not falling" (p. 82); "Yes, it's night" (p. 108).[19] The stage directions for the end of Act I indicate that the audience shall unequivocally see that night has fallen, the moon has come out, and thus Godot will not arrive. Essentially the same di-rections are found at the end of Act II. Still, none of this corrects the lingering sense of haziness and somnambulism.[20]

Just as the temporal designations of the play remain vague, so also do the geographical designations. Although the stage directions tell us that the play takes place "somewhere on a (public) road" and the dialogue suggests that this road tra-verses land belonging to Pozzo, the exact locality of this property remains indefinite. True, the characters refer to past events as hav-ing taken place in France (the Eiffel Tower [p. 10]; the Durance [p. 63]; the Vaucluse [p. 71]; the Ariège [p. 93]; and in Lucky's speech certain departments and provinces of France are mentioned). However, the use of fictitious place names (Marne-et-Oise, Merdecluse) supports the notion that the play has no specific locale.[21] Rather, it suggests a no man's land, and its effect is to universalize the "action" of the play.

In conclusion, then, the picture of man that emerges from these considerations, together with those of the first two chapters, is a nihilistic one. Man's use of reason, his senses, and his memory results in a skepticism about his identity as well as that of others, about time and about place, in short, about the cosmos. Since man has multiple identities and no clear vision of self, he cannot position himself in time. Rather, he tends to adopt the temporal mode that best suits the immediate situation. Thus, he is not only unable to arrive at a unified conception of himself, but the mere conceptualization of time collapses, and the past and the future merge with the present. The anguish of this impasse is eloquently expressed in Pozzo's violent outburst on time:

Vous n'avez pas fini de m'empoisonner avec vos histoires de temps? C'est insensé! Quand! Quand! un jour, ça ne vous suffit pas, un jour pareil aux autres, il est devenu muet, un jour je suis devenu aveugle, un jour nous deviendrons sourds, un jour nous sommes nés, un jour nous mourrons, le même jour, le même instant, ça ne vous suffit pas? (*Plus posément.*) Elles accouchent à cheval sur une tombe, la jour brille un instant, puis c'est la nuit à nouveau. (*Il tire sur la corde.*) En avant! (p. 104)

[Have you not done tormenting me with your accursed time! It's abominable! When! When! One day, is that not enough for you, one day he went dumb, one day I went blind, one day we'll go deaf, one day we were born, one day we shall die, the same day, the same second, is that not enough for you? (*Calmer.*) They give birth astride of a grave, the light gleams an instant, then it's night once more. (*He jerks the rope.*) On! (p. 57A)]

Man's finitude—reflected in the above passage and examined in the foregoing discussion of memory and its implications in respect to identity, time, and place—sets him in what could be called a tragic predicament, a predicament that obtains regardless of time or place.

4

COMMUNICATION

A key passage in *En attendant Godot* contains the following choric exchange between Vladimir and Estragon:

> *Estragon:* En attendant, essayons de converser sans nous exalter, puisque nous sommes incapables de nous taire.
> *Vladimir:* C'est vrai, nous sommes intarissables.
> *Estragon:* C'est pour ne pas penser.
> *Vladimir:* Nous avons des excuses.
> *Estragon:* C'est pour ne pas entendre.
> *Vladimir:* Nous avons nos raisons.
> *Estragon:* Toutes les voix mortes.
> *Vladimir:* Ça fait un bruit d'ailes.
> *Estragon:* De feuilles.
> *Vladimir:* De sable.
> *Estragon:* De feuilles.
>
> *Silence.*
>
> *Vladimir:* Elles parlent toutes en même temps.
> *Estragon:* Chacune à part soi.
>
> *Silence.*
>
> *Vladimir:* Plutôt elles chuchotent.
> *Estragon:* Elles murmurent.
> *Vladimir:* Elles bruissent.
>
> *Silence.*
>
> *Vladimir:* Que disent-elles?
> *Estragon:* Elles parlent de leur vie.
> *Vladimir:* Il ne leur suffit pas d'avoir vécu.

Estragon: Il faut qu'elles en parlent.
Vladimir: Il ne leur suffit pas d'être mortes.
Estragon: Ce n'est pas assez. [p. 72]

[*Estragon:* In the meantime let us try and converse calmly, since we
    are incapable of keeping silent.
Vladimir: You're right, we're inexhaustible.
Estragon: It's so we won't think.
Vladimir: We have that excuse.
Estragon: It's so we won't hear.
Vladimir: We have our reasons.
Estragon: All the dead voices.
Vladimir: They make a noise like wings.
Estragon: Like leaves.
Vladimir: Like sand.
Estragon: Like leaves.
    Silence.
Vladimir: They all speak at once.
Estragon: Each one to itself.
    Silence.
Vladimir: Rather they whisper.
Estragon: They rustle.
Vladimir: They murmur.
Estragon: They rustle.
    Silence.
Vladimir: What do they say?
Estragon: They talk about their lives.
Vladimir: To have lived is not enough for them.
Estragon: They have to talk about it.
Vladimir: To be dead is not enough for them.
Estragon: It's not sufficient. (pp. 40–40A)]

The implications of this passage are that speech is the proof of
existence as well as a manner of contending with silence, solitude,
and death. The suggestion is that the sounds (voices) of nature transcend death and by extension that speech, man's unique heritage,
transcends the tomb. Yet the play taken as a whole points out a
paradox—speech, like the body and the mind (especially the rational processes and memory), is a faulty and inadequate tool. Speech,

another mark of man's finitude, breaks down within the individual. Moreover, it sometimes leads to deterioration and often to total failure of communication with others.[1] Thus, the disintegration of societal patterns is not prevented by the force of language. In fact, seldom is there a true exchange among the characters of the play. Rather they engage in monologues that are scarcely attended to by the "listeners," or else they participate in mere games that revolve around language.

Since Beckett must use language to show the function of language in human existence, the speech patterns of the characters—recurrent vocabulary, pronoun shifts, sound effects, etc.—reenforce the major themes and the mixed tone of the play. In other words, the comic effects of the language used by the characters (i.e., by Beckett) grimly underline the themes of tedium and absurdity that dominate the play. The phrase "on attend Godot," which appears at frequent intervals, not only incorporates these themes of tedium and absurdity, but through the presence of the pronoun "on," universalizes the play, transposing the situation from the characters ("on"="nous" or "we") to the audience ("on"="tout le monde" or "everyone").[2]

While it would be difficult to demonstrate which comes first, memory deterioration or language disintegration, one clearly accompanies the other. Thus, in Lucky's case a traumatized memory is combined with partial aphasia and ultimately total silence. This condition manifests itself in stuttering (acacacacadémie; anthropopopométrie [p. 52]), in stammering (établi tabli tabli; ce qui suit qui suit qui suit; inachevés inachevés; que l'homme enfin bref que l'homme en bref; tels tels tels; les sports les sports; d'automne d'automne; la tête la tête la tête; Conard Conard [pp. 52–53]), and in a breakdown in syntax everywhere evident in his discourse.[3] The horror we experience upon hearing Lucky's speech is both social and metaphysical. His relationship to Pozzo, which allows him to speak only when invited to, has stifled his ability to coordinate language and thought. Whatever coordination might be discerned at the beginning of his tirade is anything but evident by the end. Because of the decomposition of this skill taking place within the context of Lucky's thinkpiece, it is not surprising that in Act II Lucky has gone totally dumb.

On yet another level the horror of Lucky's linguistic predicament is even more intense. Some might argue that the mild scatology of "caca" and "popo" contained in his particular articulation of the words "académie" and "anthropométrie" is comic. But the pathological nature of Lucky's speech is in the final analysis quite distressing; for the act of speaking is that which gives man dignity and demonstrates his ability to think logically and coherently. But if this speech seems terrible, what is more terrible (if one does not happen to be a nihilist) is the prolonged solitude and silence in which Lucky, like all men, is finally engulfed. Because of this, he provides an extreme contrast to the chattering and aimless rambling of the other three characters.

Even though so extreme a breakdown does not occur in the speech of the other characters, they too give some evidence of a certain amount of speech disintegration. Ellipsis and stammering are observable in Pozzo's speech from the stress of Vladimir's criticism: "Je n'en peux plus . . . plus supporter . . . ce qu'il fait . . . pouvez pas savoir . . . c'est affreux . . . faut qu'il s'en aille . . . (Il brandit le bras) . . . je deviens fou . . . (Il s'effondre, la tête dans les bras.) Je n'en peux plus . . . peux plus . . ." (p. 39) ["I can't bear it . . . any longer . . . the way he goes on . . . you've no idea . . . it's terrible . . . he must go . . . (he waves his arms) . . . I'm going mad . . . (He collapses, his head in his hands) . . . I can't bear it . . . any longer . . ." (pp. 22A–23).]. A bit later he exhibits similar speech patterns as a result of the emotion he experiences in talking about how Lucky used to be in comparison with his present condition: "Autrefois . . . il était gentil . . . il m'aidait . . . me distrayait . . . il me rendait meilleur . . . maintenant . . . il m'assassine . . ." (p. 39) ["He used to be so kind . . . so helpful . . . and entertaining . . . my good angel . . . and now . . . he's killing me" (p. 23).].

Estragon displays certain speech eruptions that Germaine Brée describes as baby talk (pp. 20, 35, n. 103), and since Estragon has some infantile personality traits this is perhaps justified. However, this breakdown in Estragon's speech occurs when there is a lack of comprehension on the part of his listener. Thus, he struggles to explain why he cannot commit suicide ahead of the uncomprehending Vladimir: "Gogo leger—branche pas casser—Gogo mort.

Didi lourd—branche casser—Didi seul" (p. 20) ["Gogo light—
bough not break—Gogo dead. Didi heavy—bough break—Didi
alone" (p. 12A).]. It is not so much that, as Brée puts it, "the intellectual effort to explain is too much for Estragon" (p. 20, n. 36),
but, rather, that in his frustration he is oversimplifying his explanation as a father might with a small son. [4]

The same abbreviated speech occurs again when once more in
frustration Estragon breaks down his often repeated question
"Pourquoi ne dépose-t-il pas ses bagages?" ("Why doesn't he put
down his baggage?") into its bare essentials, as if this method of
interrogation would give better results: "Bagages! (*Il pointe son
doigt vers Lucky.*) Pourquoi? Toujours tenir. (*Il fait celui qui ploie,
en haletant.*) Jamais déposer. (*Il ouvre les mains, se redresse avec
soulagement.*) Pourquoi?" (p. 35) ["Bags. (*He points at Lucky.*)
Why? Always hold. (*He sags, panting.*) Never put down. (*He opens
his hands, straightens up with relief.*) Why?" (p. 21)].

Hesitancy in speech is observable in both Estragon and Vladimir.
In the former this fumbling for words appears to emanate from em-
barrassment ("C'est-à-dire . . . l'obscurité . . . la fatigue . . . la faib-
lesse . . . l'attente . . . j'avoue . . . j'ai cru . . . un instant . . ." [pp.
26–27]) ["That's to say . . . you understand . . . the dusk . . . the
strain . . . waiting . . . I confess . . . I imagined . . . for a second
. . ." (p. 16).] or from the fear of rejection ("Heu . . . vous ne man-
gez pas . . . heu . . . vous n'avez plus besoin . . . des os . . . Mon-
seur?" [p. 31]) ["Er . . . you've finished with the . . . er . . . you
don't need the . . . er . . . bones, Sir?" (p. 18).]. Vladimir on the
other hand gropes for words when he has difficulty remembering
what he was talking about: "Attends . . . on s'est embrassé . . . on
était content . . . content . . . qu' est-ce qu'on fait maintenant qu'on
est content . . . on attend . . . voyons . . . ça vient . . . on attend
. . . maintenant qu'on est content . . . on attend . . . voyons . . .
ah! L'arbre!" (p. 75) ["Wait . . . we embraced . . . we were happy
. . . happy . . . what do we do now that we're happy . . . go on
waiting . . . waiting . . . let me think . . . it's coming . . . go on
waiting . . . now that we're happy . . . let me see . . . ah! The tree!"
(p. 42).]. Here is clear evidence of the connection between speech
disintegration and faulty memory. Vladimir exhibits a similar difficulty in formulating his speech when he must answer the boy's

question "Qu'est-ce que je dois dire à Monsieur Godot?" ["What
am I to tell Mr. Godot, Sir?"], a question for which Vladimir has
no preconceived answer: "Tu lui diras—*(il s'interrompt)*—tu lui
diras que tu m'as vu et que—*(il réfléchit)*—que tu m'as vu. *(Un
temps. Vladimir s'avance, le garçon recule, Vladimir s'arrête.)* Dis,
tu es bien sûr de m'avoir vu, tu ne vas pas me dire demain que tu
ne m'as jamais vu?" (p. 107) ["Tell him . . . *(he hesitates)* . . . that
you saw me and that . . . *(he hesitates)* . . . that you saw me.
*(Pause. Vladimir advances, the boy recoils. Vladimir halts, the boy
halts. With sudden violence.)* You're sure you saw me, you won't
come and tell me to-morrow that you never saw me!" (p. 59).]. Vladimir also reveals linguistic hesitance and compensation occurring
because his thoughts appear to be ahead of his speech: "Après en
avoir sucé la substance vous le jetez comme un . . . *(il cherche)*
. . . comme une peau de banane. Avouez que . . ." (p. 39) ["After
having sucked all the good out of him you chuck him away like a
. . . like a banana skin. Really . . ." (p. 22A).]. Language disintegration such as this on the individual level is a sign of the general
inadequacy of speech to cope with a variety of situations and of the
incoordination between speech and memory or thought.

Speech disintegration within the individual at the level of monologue already spells out the limitations of language, but when the
individual is attempting to carry on a dialogue with others the limitations of language become even more apparent. These limitations
result in a breakdown in communication (present in the monologue
but rampant in the dialogue), and the whole process serves only to
reenforce the solitude that is the fundamental lot of each of the
characters.

One of the major causes of misunderstanding among the characters proceeds from faulty communication due to types of imprecision such as ambiguity, misconstruing a question, confusion of
sounds, etc. The play opens on an ambiguous note, "Nothing to be
done" ("Rien à faire"), that does not lead into a dialogue but into
two monologues—Estragon discussing his shoes, Vladimir their tedious existence and their inability to alter it. Again, misunderstanding arises from ambiguous syntax when Pozzo asks "Êtes-vous des
amis?" ("Are you friends?"). Estragon interprets this to mean "Are
you and Vladimir friends?," and Vladimir has to explain that Pozzo

is asking whether Vladimir and Estragon are friends of his ("Non, il veut dire des amis à lui" [p. 97]). Other forms of imprecision also play roles in faulty communication. On one occasion Estragon forces Vladimir to be more explicit:

> Vladimir (piqué): Alors pourquoi rappliquer?
> Estragon: Je ne sais pas.
> Vladimir: Mais moi je le sais. Parce que tu ne sais pas te défendre.
> Moi je ne t'aurais pas laissé battre.
> Estragon: Tu n'aurais pas pu l'empêcher.
> Vladimir: Pourquoi?
> Estragon: Ils étaient dix.
> Vladimir: Mais non, je veux dire que je t'aurais empêché de t'exposer à être battu. (p. 68)[5]

> [Vladimir: (vexed). Then why do you always come crawling back?
> Estragon: I don't know.
> Vladimir: No, but I do. It's because you don't know how to defend yourself. I wouldn't have let them beat you.
> Estragon: You couldn't have stopped them.
> Vladimir: Why not?
> Estragon: There were ten of them.
> Vladimir: No, I mean before they beat you. I would have stopped you from doing whatever it was you were doing. (p. 38A)]

A very complex misunderstanding arising from a faulty pronominal reference takes place between Estragon and Vladimir. Vladimir without prompting says, "Si tu les essayais" ("Suppose you try them?"), using a specific pronoun ("les") without any specified reference. Estragon retorts to this proposal by saying that he has tried everything ("J'ai tout essayé"). His abstract, all-inclusive pronoun, "tout," is no clearer than Vladimir's "les," but it forces Vladimir to explain that he means the shoes (p. 79).

An additional example of ambiguity leading to a breakdown in communication occurs in the passage where Pozzo asks Vladimir what is keeping Estragon from acting ("Qu'est ce qu'il attend?" [p. 101].). Vladimir in turn says to Estragon, "Qu'est-ce que tu attends?" and Estragon, misunderstanding the immediate application of the verb "attendre," answers "J'attends Godot."

> [Pozzo: Yes, yes, let your friend go, he stinks so. (Silence.) What is he waiting for?

Vladimir: What you waiting for?
Estragon: I'm waiting for Godot. (p. 56)]

The misunderstanding of this particular verb is of utmost significance, for it relates to one of the major themes of the play. In a
passage not present in the English version of the play still another
misunderstanding occurs when Estragon responds to what was obviously a rhetorical question on the part of Pozzo:

> *Pozzo:* Ou je ne lui demande rien. Bon. Ne m'interrompez pas.
> Mettons que je lui demande de . . . danser, par exemple. Qu'est-
> ce qui se produit?
> *Estragon:* Il se met à siffler.
> *Pozzo (fâché):* Je ne dirai plus rien. (p. 49)

> *Paraphrased:* [Pozzo asks what they think might happen if he re-
> quested that Lucky dance, and Estragon answers this obviously
> rhetorical question by speculating that Lucky will whistle. This
> infuriates Pozzo, who then pouts and says he won't say anything
> more.]

Finally, the humor of a situation is heightened by phonological
malentendu. At the end of the play, for example, Vladimir must
reiterate with emphasis his "Relève ton pantalon," which Estragon
has misunderstood as "enlève ton pantalon" (p. 109).[6]

These linguistic accidents are a source of humor in the play, as
they would be in any conventional comedy. However, they, like
other factors in *En attendant Godot,* point out what is in reality a
crucial aspect of man's finitude: in this case, his inability to communicate to others his ideas about himself and the world.

This inability is also pictured through the play's almost endless
monologues that illustrate the characters' egocentricity (shown by
their desire to dominate the conversation and their inattention to
what is being said to them). These monologues, which reveal the
essential solitude of the characters, are of several varieties: the monologue (or soliloquy) per se, the monologue delivered by one character in the midst of a conversation between two others, and two
or three characters' simultaneously indulging in a monologue.

The most obvious example of monologue in the play is Lucky's
speech, which is entirely special, because it is delivered upon command, and is therefore to some extent less characteristic of the

egocentricity discussed above. Since it is offered as a diversion, it is, instead, a reflection of the use of monologue as a theatrical device.

Pozzo's monologues, on the other hand, proceed largely from his egocentricity (e.g., his not wanting to be interrupted [p. 49]), although they are, in addition, also intended as divertissements. This latter point is especially true of his diatribe on how the night falls (pp. 43–44). Interestingly, no monologues are delivered by Pozzo and Lucky in Act II, and, given the theatrical origins of these monologues, their absence suggests that the theater as diversion is dead.

Vladimir's use of monologue is like Pozzo's in that it is often egocentric in nature, but unlike Pozzo's in that it is not theatrical and also because it reflects an interior rumination that is consistent with his rational temperament. (See Fr., pp. 91, 105; Eng., pp. 51, 58).[7] He is the one character who most appears to be thinking out loud and to be commenting on human nature and human existence. As Ruby Cohn has pointed out, his very nickname, "Didi," suggests the French words "dis, dis" (a command form of the French verb *dire* meaning to say or to tell),[8] hence, his tendency to verbalize his thought, which is given to the abstract.

Partial conversation disintegration occurs when one character sustains his own subject of conversation while two others are carrying on a coherent discussion between themselves. Such is the case when Vladimir, finding himself on the ground with Pozzo, engages in a conversation with Estragon about going to the Ariège while Pozzo unsuccessfully tries to get their attention.

Vladimir: Aide-moi!
Estragon: Moi, je m'en vais.
Vladimir: Aide-moi d'abord. Puis nous partirons ensemble.
Estragon: Tu le promets?
Vladimir: Je le jure!
Estragon: Et nous ne reviendrons jamais.
Vladimir: Jamais!
Estragon: Nous irons dans l'Ariège.
Vladimir: Où tu voudras.
Pozzo: Trois cents! Quatre cents!
Estragon: J'ai toujours voulu me ballader dans l'Ariège.
Vladimir: Tu t'y balladeras. (p. 93)[9]

Total disintegration in conversation occurs when the characters
conduct simultaneous monologues. In some cases this involves only
two characters, as in the passage where, directly following Pozzo's
remark that there has been an increase in the population ("Il est
vrai que la population a augmenté"), which in itself has little or
nothing to do with what he has just been saying about the relative
merits of our epoch, Vladimir says, "Essaie de marcher" ("Try to
walk"), after which Pozzo asks if they know who taught him all these
"beautiful things" ("Savez-vous qui m'a appris toutes ces belles
choses?"), and, pointing to Lucky, adds, "He did" ("Lui" [p. 38]).
These monologues continue for several lines until Vladimir asks
what a knouk is ("Qu'est-ce que c'est, un knouk?" [p. 39]), and finally they arrive at an exchange concerning the word "knouk."
Some conversations appear to be double monologues, but in reality
necessary transitions simply have been omitted by the speaker. An
example of this is Estragon's claim that his left lung is weak but his
right one is in perfect shape ("Mon poumon gauche est très fai-
ble. . . . Mais mon poumon droit est en parfait état!"), which is
vaguely related to Pozzo's exclamation when he loses his pipe ("J'ai
perdu mon pulvérisateur!") and is intended to suggest that he too,
like Pozzo, might need an atomizer (p. 47).
Absolute chaos results when all three characters are engaged in
simultaneous monologues, as in the following passage:

Estragon: Nous naissons tous fous. Quelques-uns le demeurent.
Pozzo: Au secours, je vous donnerai de l'argent!
Estragon: Combien?
Pozzo: Cent francs.
Estragon: Ce n'est pas assez.
Vladimir: Je n'irais pas jusque-là.
Estragon: Tu trouves que c'est assez?
Vladimir: Non, je veux dire jusqu'à affirmer que je n'avais pas toute
  ma tête en venant au monde. Mais la question n'est pas là.
Pozzo: Deux cents.
Vladimir: Nous attendons. Nous nous ennuyons. (*Il lève la main*).
  Non, ne proteste pas, nous nous ennuyons ferme, c'est incontest-
  able. Bon. Une diversion se présente et que faisons-nous? Nous
  la laissons pourrir. Allons, au travail. (*Il avance vers Pozzo, s'arrête*).
  Dans un instant, tout se disipera, nous serons à nouveau seuls, au
  milieu des solitudes. (*Il rêve*).

Pozzo: Deux cents!
Vladimir: On arrive.
Il essaie de soulever Pozzo, n'y arrive pas, renouvelle ses efforts,
trébuche dans les bagages, tombe, essaie de se relever, n'y arrive
pas.
Estragon: Qu'est-ce vous avez tous?
Vladimir: Au secours!
Estragon: Je m'en vais.
Vladimir: Ne m'abandonne pas! Ils me tueront!
Pozzo: Où suis-je?
Vladimir: Gogo!
Pozzo: A moi.
Vladimir: Aide-moi! (pp. 92–93)

[*Estragon:* . . . We are all born mad. Some remain so.
Pozzo: Help! I'll pay you!
Estragon: How much?
Pozzo: One hundred francs!
Estragon: It's not enough.
Vladimir: I wouldn't go so far as that.
Estragon: You think it's enough?
Vladimir: No, I mean so far as to assert that I was weak in the head
   when I came into the world. But that is not the question.
Pozzo: Two hundred!
Vladimir: We wait. We are bored. (*He throws up his hand.*) No, don't
   protest, we are bored to death, there's no denying it. Good. A
   diversion comes along and what do we do? We let it go to waste.
   Come, let's get to work! (*He advances towards the heap, stops in
   his stride.*) In an instant all will vanish and we'll be alone once
   more, in the midst of nothingness! *He broods.*
Pozzo: Two hundred!
Vladimir: We're coming!
   He tries to pull Pozzo to his feet, fails, tries again, stumbles, falls,
   tries to get up, fails.
Estragon: What's the matter with you all?
Vladimir: Help!
Estragon: I'm going.
Vladimir: Don't leave me! They'll kill me!
Pozzo: Where am I?
Vladimir: Gogo!
Pozzo: Help!
Vladimir: Help! (pp. 51A–52A)]

These simultaneous monologues tell much about man's frequent inability to sustain a conversation because of his egocentricity, which is manifested in the pressing desire to express his own thoughts and in his inattentiveness to the discourse of others. Indeed, because of this inattentiveness, one person is forced to repeat a given question several times before he receives an answer. Thus Estragon must ask Vladimir several times if they are tied to Godot (p. 22 ff.); he must ask Pozzo repeatedly why Lucky does not put down his bags (p. 29 ff.); and Vladimir asks Pozzo seven times in rapid succession if he wants to get rid of Lucky ("Vous voulez vous en debarrasser?" [p. 36].).

In contrast to these forms of conversation disintegration, many passages occur that *appear* to represent integrated dialogue. Yet when examined closely, they are revealed to be merely mock conversations. In fact, most conversations in this category are linguistic games, intended, like other games played by Estragon and Vladimir, to kill time. This can be proved by the frequent repetition of such sentences as "yes, let's have a conversation" ("C'est ça, faisons un peu de conversation" [p. 57].), and, "Yes, let's ask each other questions" ("C'est ça, posons-nous des questions" [p. 74].), which appear to occur as a type of fuel intended to keep the "dialogue" moving. At the end of a linguistic exchange, the sentences suggest the success of a spurt of conversation ("Ce n'était pas si mal comme petit galop" [p. 75]) or the impression the conversation gives them of being alive ("On trouve toujours quelque chose, hein, Didi, pour nous donner l'impression d'exister?" [p. 79].). Such sentences clearly establish that Estragon and Vladimir regard their conversations not only as games but as efforts to prove that they exist, so long as they keep talking.[10] This being so, the subject matter of the conversation is of no importance to them:

> Vladimir: Dis quelque chose!
> Estragon: Je cherche.
>
> Long silence.
>
> Vladimir (angoissé): Dis n'importe quoi!
> Estragon: Qu'est-ce qu'on fait maintenant?
> Vladimir: On attend Godot.
> Estragon: C'est vrai.
>
> Silence.
>
> Vladimir: Ce que c'est difficile!

Estragon: Si tu chantais?
Vladimir: Non non (*Il cherche.*) On n'a qu'à recommencer.
Estragon: Ça ne me semble pas bien difficile en effet.
Vladimir: C'est le départ qui est difficile.
Estragon: On peut partir de n'importe quoi.
Vladimir: Oui, mais il faut se décider.
Estragon: C'est vrai. (p. 73)

[*Vladimir:* Say something!
Estragon: I'm trying.
                                                              Long silence.

Vladimir (in anguish): Say anything at all!
Estragon: What do we do now?
Vladimir: Wait for Godot.
Estragon: Ah!
                                                                  Silence.

Vladimir: This is awful!
Estragon: Sing something.
Vladimir: No no! (*He reflects.*) We could start all over again perhaps.
Estragon: That should be easy.
Vladimir: It's the start that's difficult.
Estragon: You can start from anything.
Vladimir: Yes, but you have to decide.
Estragon: True. (pp. 40A–41)]

The last few sentences of the above passage express the idea that the most difficult thing about having a conversation is getting started.

These requests for conversation contrast with the interruptions that occur when one character is irritated or bored by another's subject matter, thereby deterring the free flow of conversation. Thus, Estragon tells Vladimir that enough has been said about the shoes (p. 80), and Vladimir cuts off Estragon's bawdy story with an emphatic "That's enough!" (p. 19). Vladimir also interrupts both of Estragon's efforts to recount his dreams, first with an exclamation telling him not to tell about them (p. 17) and later with a command that he say nothing (p. 81). Pozzo, on the other hand, introduces a subject of conversation and cuts off any potential response from Vladimir or Estragon by insisting that they not talk about it (p. 38).

Despite these conversation-stoppers, all of the conversations are motivated by the characters' desire simply to keep talking, no matter how trivial the subject. That these empty conversations are habitual with Vladimir and Estragon is clearly recognized by Estragon who, when Vladimir asks him what they were talking about last night, responds, "Oh . . . à bâtons rompus peut-être, à propos de bottes. (*Avec assurance.*) Voilà, je me rappelle, hier soir nous avons bavardé, à propos de bottes. Il y a un demi-siècle que ça dure" (p. 76). ["Oh . . . this and that I suppose, nothing in particular. (*With assurance.*) Yes, now I remember, yesterday evening we spent blathering about nothing in particular. That's been going on now for half a century" (p. 42A)].

Thus, in their need to continue talking, Vladimir and Estragon invent various kinds of games using language as their medium. One of the kinds of language games that the two play involves punning, as when Estragon plays on the word "saule" (willow) by saying that weeping will cease ("Finis les pleurs" [p. 15].). Other examples of this, not readily translatable, include Estragon's puns on the words "retenir" (hold back, p. 41) and "bottes" (boots or this and that, in the passage just above, p. 76); Vladimir's triple pun on the word "plateau" (stage, dished up, plateau, p. 85) and on the word "tomber" (to fall, to happen at just the right time, p. 88). Although the presence of puns in a comedy comes as no surprise, most of these puns are built on grim themes, which is in keeping with the mixed genres of this play.

The vaudeville routines of Estragon and Vladimir are, however, more important than the puns as language games, owing to their greater frequency and to their being linked to the main themes of the play both by their content and by the contrast they provide to the otherwise slow-moving tempo of the play. (Thus, contradictory principles of rhythm reflect the temporal ironies in human existence.) The most obvious characteristics of these passages are the rhythmical pattern and the play on sound. In addition they often appear to represent a striving for the *mot juste*, thus the exchange (p. 16) as to whether the tree should be called an *arbuste* (bush) or an *arbrisseau* (shrubby tree). These characteristics have led Germaine Brée to call this special type of dialogue "cumulative patter" (p. 5), thus relegating it to the realm of vaudeville or the music hall.

This is a perfectly accurate description up to a point, but since such dialogue reflects the themes of the play, and for other reasons to be discussed in Chapter Six, they function much as the chorus in a Greek tragedy (or comedy?) does. Like some of the Greek choric interludes, exposition is provided by one of these routines, excerpts from which follow:

Vladimir: Attendons voir ce qu'il va nous dire.
Estragon: Qui?
Vladimir: Godot.
Estragon: Voilà.
Vladimir: Attendons d'être fixés d'abord.
Estragon: D'un autre côté, on ferait peut-être mieux de battre le fer avant qu'il soit glacé.
Vladimir: Je suis curieux de savoir ce qu'il va nous dire. Ça ne nous engage à rien.
Estragon: Qu'est-ce qu'on lui a demandé au juste? . . .
Vladimir: Eh bien . . . Rien de bien précis.
Estragon: Une sorte de prière.
Vladimir: Voilà.
Estragon: Une vague supplique.
Vladimir: Si tu veux.
Estragon: Et qu'a-t-il répondu?
Vladimir: Qu'il verrait.
Estragon: Qu'il ne pouvait rien promettre.
Vladimir: Qu'il lui fallait réfléchir. . . . Consulter sa famille.
Estragon: Ses amis.
Vladimir: Ses agents.
Estragon: Ses correspondants.
Vladimir: Ses registres.
Estragon: Son compte en banque.
Vladimir: Avant de se prononcer.
Estragon: C'est normal.
Vladimir: N'est-ce pas?
Estragon: Il me semble.
Vladimir: A moi aussi. (pp. 20–21)

[*Vladimir:* Let's wait and see what he says.
Estragon: Who?
Vladimir: Godot.
Estragon: Good idea.

Vladimir: Let's wait till we know exactly how we stand.
Estragon: On the other hand it might be better to strike the iron
   before it freezes.
Vladimir: I'm curious to hear what he has to offer. Then we'll take
   it or leave it.
Estragon: What exactly did we ask him for? . . .
Vladimir: Oh . . . Nothing very definite.
Estragon: A kind of prayer.
Vladimir: Precisely.
Estragon: A vague supplication.
Vladimir: Exactly.
Estragon: And what did he reply?
Vladimir: That he'd see.
Estragon: That he couldn't promise anything.
Vladimir: That he'd have to think it over.
Estragon: In the quiet of his home.
Vladimir: Consult his family.
Estragon: His friends.
Vladimir: His agents.
Estragon: His correspondents.
Vladimir: His books.
Estragon: His bank account.
Vladimir: Before taking a decision.
Estragon: It's the normal thing.
Vladimir: Is it not?
Estragon: I think it is.
Vladimir: I think so too. (pp. 12A–13)]

Still more significantly, this type of repartee between Vladimir
and Estragon provides three different kinds of commentary: commentary on their own existential plight, commentary on the predicament of Pozzo and Lucky, and commentary on the audience.
   The quotation at the beginning of this chapter showed how one
of these routines incorporates the theme presently under discussion, the insatiable need to speak that even transcends death. Another basic necessity, that of habit, is reflected in the following
routine:

Vladimir: Question de tempérament.
Estragon: De caractère.
Vladimir: On n'y peut rien.

Estragon: On a beau se démener.
Vladimir: On reste ce qu'on est.
Estragon: On a beau se tortiller.
Vladimir: Le fond ne change pas.
Estragon: Rien à faire. (p. 24)

[*Vladimir:* Question of temperament.
Estragon: Of character.
Vladimir: Nothing you can do about it.
Estragon: No use struggling.
Vladimir: One is what one is.
Estragon: No use wriggling.
Vladimir: The essential doesn't change.
Estragon: Nothing to be done. (p. 14A)]

The last line of the above quotation aptly introduces two other motifs found in these "vaudeville routines": the search for entertainment (pp. 79, 87) and how life is habitually confronted by waiting (pp. 44, 69). Yet another of these routines, not present in the English version, embodies the current of skepticism running through the play; for Vladimir and Estragon wonder if they have really seen Pozzo and Lucky or if their appearance was a vision, or an illusion, or a hallucination, rather than a reality:

Vladimir: Ils se sont peut-être arrêtés tout simplement.
Estragon: Voilà.
Vladimir: Pour se reposer.
Estragon: Pour se restaurer.
Vladimir: Ils ont peut-être rebroussé chemin?
Estragon: Voilà.
Vladimir: C'était peut-être une vision.
Estragon: Une illusion.
Vladimir: Une hallucination.
Estragon: Une illusion. (p. 101)

In three of these vaudeville routines Vladimir and Estragon, much like a Greek chorus, comment on the "tragic" scene unfolding before them; thus, they engage in the following stichomythic exchange about the sore on Lucky's neck:

Vladimir: Regarde-moi ça!
Estragon: Quoi?
Vladimir (indiquant): Le cou.
Estragon (regardant le cou): Je ne vois rien.
Vladimir: Mets-toi ici.
　　　　　　　　　　Estragon se met à la place de Vladimir.
Estragon: En effet.
Vladimir: A vif.
Estragon: C'est la corde.
Vladimir: A force de frotter.
Estragon: Qu'est-ce que tu veux.
Vladimir: C'est le noeud.
Estragon: C'est fatal. (p. 29)

[*Vladimir:* Look!
Estragon: What?
Vladimir: (pointing). His neck!
Estragon: (looking at the neck). I see nothing.
Vladimir: Here.
　　　　　Estragon goes over beside Vladimir.
Estragon: Oh I say!
Vladimir: A running sore!
Estragon: It's the rope.
Vladimir: It's the rubbing.
Estragon: It's inevitable.
Vladimir: It's the knot.
Estragon: It's the chafing. (p. 17A)]

And the exchange continues as Vladimir and Estragon compare
notes concerning Lucky's appearance:

Vladimir: Il n'est pas mal.
Estragon: . . . Tu trouves?
Vladimir: Un peu efféminé.
Estragon: Il bave.
Vladimir: C'est forcé.
Estragon: Il écume.
Vladimir: C'est peut-être un idiot.
Estragon: Un crétin.
Vladimir: . . . On dirait un goitre.

Estragon: . . . Ce n'est pas sûr.
Vladimir: Il halète.
Estragon: C'est normal.
Vladimir: Et ses yeux!
Estragon: Qu'est-ce qu'ils ont?
Vladimir: Ils sortent. (pp. 29–30)

[*Vladimir:* . . . He's not bad looking.
Estragon: . . . Would you say so?
Vladimir: A trifle effeminate.
Estragon: Look at the slobber.
Vladimir: It's inevitable.
Estragon: Look at the slaver.
Vladimir: Perhaps he's a halfwit.
Estragon: A cretin.
Vladimir: . . . Looks like a goiter.
Estragon: . . . It's not certain.
Vladimir: He's panting.
Estragon: It's inevitable.
Vladimir: And his eyes!
Estragon: What about them?
Vladimir: Goggling out of his head. (p. 17A)]

Seeing that Pozzo is nearly at the end of his resources, the two men say to each other:

Vladimir: Il n'en peut plus.
Estragon: C'est affreux.
Vladimir: Il devient fou.
Estragon: C'est dégoûtant. (p. 39)

[*Vladimir:* He can't bear it.
Estragon: Any longer.
Vladimir: He's going mad.
Estragon: It's terrible. (p. 23)]

Finding the spectacle of Lucky and Pozzo to be a diversion in their otherwise tedious existence, they exchange observations on the scene in another of these routines:

Vladimir: Charmante soirée.
Estragon: Inoubliable.

Vladimir: Et ce n'est pas fini.
Estragon: On dirait que non.
Vladimir: Ça ne fait que commencer.
Estragon: C'est terrible.
Vladimir: On se croirait au spectacle.
Estragon: Au cirque.
Vladimir: Au music-hall.
Estragon: Au cirque. (p. 40)

[*Vladimir:* Charming evening we're having.
Estragon: Unforgettable.
Vladimir: And it's not over.
Estragon: Apparently not.
Vladimir: It's only beginning.
Estragon: It's awful.
Vladimir: Worse than the pantomime.
Estragon: The circus.
Vladimir: The music-hall.
Estragon: The circus. (pp. 23–23A)]

Finally, in one of these routines Vladimir and Estragon draw the audience into the cosmos of the play with their commentary on the spectators:

Vladimir: D'où viennent tous ces cadavres?
Estragon: Ces ossements.
Vladimir: Voilà.
Estragon: Evidemment.
Vladimir: On a dû penser un peu.
Estragon: Tout à fait au commencement.
Vladimir: Un charnier, un charnier.
Estragon: Il n'y a qu'à ne pas regarder.
Vladimir: Ça tire l'oeil.
Estragon: C'est vrai.
Vladimir: Malgré qu'on en ait.
Estragon: Comment?
Vladimir: Malgré qu'on en ait.
Estragon: Il faudrait se tourner résolument vers la nature.
Vladimir: Nous avons essayé.
Estragon: C'est vrai.
Vladimir: Oh, ce n'est pas le pire, bien sûr.

Estragon: Quoi donc?
Vladimir: D'avoir pensé.
Estragon: Evidemment.
Vladimir: Mais on s'en serait passé.
Estragon: Qu'est-ce que tu veux?
Vladimir: Je sais, je sais. (pp. 74–75)

[*Vladimir:* Where are all these corpses from?
Estragon: These skeletons.
Vladimir: Tell me that.
Estragon: True.
Vladimir: We must have thought a little.
Estragon: At the very beginning.
Vladimir: A charnel-house! A charnel-house!
Estragon: You don't have to look.
Vladimir: You can't help looking.
Estragon: True.
Vladimir: Try as one may.
Estragon: I beg your pardon?
Vladimir: Try as one may.
Estragon: We should turn resolutely towards Nature.
Vladimir: We've tried that.
Estragon: True.
Vladimir: Oh it's not the worst, I know.
Estragon: What?
Vladimir: To have thought.
Estragon: Obviously.
Vladimir: But we could have done without it.
Estragon: Que voulez-vous?
Vladimir: I beg your pardon?
Estragon: Que voulez-vous.
Vladimir: Ah! que voulez-vous. Exactly. (pp. 41A–42)]

If these vaudeville routines do indeed have something in common with the functions of the ancient Greek chorus, then their significance here is that modern man, who is anything but a conventional hero, is forced into a position of universalizing his own "tragic" position. The implication of all this is that his state of solitude is so profound that society is not present to comment meaningfully upon his deeds, to praise and to forewarn, and to incorporate him into the mainstream or to exile him, as the case may be. Yet, whatever additional functions these routines have, their major purpose is to demonstrate the trivial and playful use of language by Vladimir and Estragon (as well as by us) as one of the principal ways of passing time. This is quite obvious since the passage just quoted from the play is directly followed by a period of silence, after which Estragon says "Ce n'était pas si mal comme petit galop," to which Vladimir replies, "Oui, mais maintenant il va falloir trouver autre chose," and the two men strive desperately to find a new subject of "conversation":

> *Estragon:* Voyons.
> *Vladimir:* Voyons.
> *Estragon:* Voyons.
> *Ils réfléchissent.*
> *Vladimir:* Qu'est-ce que je disais? On pourrait reprendre là. (p. 75)

> [*Estragon:* That wasn't such a bad little canter.
> *Vladimir:* Yes, but now we'll have to find something else.
> *Estragon:* Let me see.
>   (*He takes off his hat, concentrates.*)
> *Estragon:* Let me see. . . .
> *Vladimir:* Let me see. . . .
>   (*Long silence.*) Ah! . . .
> *Estragon:* Well?
> *Vladimir:* What was I saying, we could go on from there. (p. 42)]

As the atmosphere of tedium becomes more intense in Act II of *En attendant Godot*, the number of games increases, as a result of which the refrain,

> *Estragon:* Allons-nous-en.
> *Vladimir:* On ne peut pas.
> *Estragon:* Pourquoi?
> *Vladimir:* On attend Godot.
> *Estragon:* C'est vrai.

> [*Estragon:* Let's go.
> *Vladimir:* We can't.

> *Estragon:* Why not?
> *Vladimir:* We're waiting for Godot.
> *Estragon:* Ah! (p. 50)]

which appears infrequently in Act I (pp. 15, 57), is repeated again
and again in Act II (pp. 69, 73, 78, 81, 89, 97). This fixed linguistic
pattern appears to be a demarcation indicating that at the moment
Vladimir and Estragon have run out of material, but, because they
remember that they must bide their time while waiting for Godot,
they realize that the games must continue. The formulaic nature of
this exchange suggests that it is a habitual language pattern. Certainly the presence of Estragon's "C'est vrai" ("That's true" or "Ah!")
in this refrain justifies calling it habitual, for this phrase is a speech
tic with Estragon, appearing many times independent of the refrain
(pp. 95, 98). Of course, this phrase is used by the other characters
as well (Pozzo, p. 43; Vladimir, p. 100) and points up a central irony
in the use of phrases of this sort since the play demonstrates that
one cannot know what truth is (See again Vladimir's "Mais dans tout
cela, qu'y aura-t-il de vrai?" [p. 105]. In English he asks what truth
there will be in all that [p. 58].).

"C'est vrai" ("That's true") is not the only example of cliché language appearing in the play. The characters insert such phrases as
"you see?" ("voyez-vous?" [pp. 27, 28].), "What do you expect?"
("Que voulez-vous?" [pp. 30, 32].), which contribute nothing to the
meaning of the dialogue but which by their humdrum nature support the theme of tedium found in the play. Upon occasion, however, a fixed phrase may trigger a conversational digression. Such
is the case with Vladimir's "du calme" (p. 18), which stimulates
Estragon to remember how the English pronounce the word "calm"
and subsequently a bawdy story having to do with an Englishman.

In short, linguistic or conversational tedium alternates with linguistic or conversational chaos.

The characters in *En attendant Godot* demonstrate the tendency
human beings have not only to use language to pass time or play
games, but also to put it to affective and ceremonial uses in inap-
propriate circumstances, thus providing a glimpse of the extent to
which language can render the human being comic if not absurd.
Such is the case with the monosyllabic "do do do do" of Vladimir's

lullaby,[11] obviously baby talk (for sleep), which offers an ironic
because feeble solution to the world of insomnia and nightmare en-
veloping the characters. The following ceremonious dialogue among
Vladimir, Estragon, and Pozzo is in intentionally strong contrast to
the picture of a crumbling civilization that has just been portrayed
through the relationship between Lucky and Pozzo:[12]

Estragon: Alors adieu.
Pozzo: Adieu.
Vladimir: Adieu.
Estragon: Adieu.

                                        Silence. Personne ne bouge.

Vladimir: Adieu.
Pozzo: Adieu.
Estragon: Adieu.

                                                  Silence.

Pozzo: Et merci.
Vladimir: Merci à vous.
Pozzo: De rien.
Estragon: Mais si.
Pozzo: Mais non.
Vladimir: Mais si.
Estragon: Mais non. (p. 56)

[*Estragon:* Then adieu.
Pozzo: Adieu.
Vladimir: Adieu.
Pozzo: Adieu.

                                        Silence. No one moves.

Vladimir: Adieu.
Pozzo: Adieu.
Estragon: Adieu.

                                                  Silence.

Pozzo: And thank you.
Vladimir: Thank *you.*
Pozzo: Not at all.
Estragon: Yes yes.
Pozzo: No no.
Vladimir: Yes yes.
Estragon: No no. (p. 31)]

Another example of protocol language, occurring this time between
Vladimir and Estragon, is not in keeping with their respective tendency toward monologue and basic egocentricity:[13]

> *Vladimir:* Oh pardon!
> *Estragon:* Je t'écoute.
> *Vladimir:* Mais non!
> *Estragon:* Mais si!
> *Vladimir:* Je t'ai coupé.
> *Estragon:* Au contraire.
> > *Il se regardent avec colère.*
> *Vladimir:* Voyons, pas de cérémonie.
> *Estragon:* Ne sois pas têtu, voyons.
> *Vladimir (avec force):* Achève ta phrase, je te dis.
> *Estragon (de même):* Achève la tienne. (p. 86)

> [*Vladimir:* Oh pardon!
> *Estragon:* Carry on.
> *Vladimir:* No no, after you.
> *Estragon:* No no, you first.
> *Vladimir:* I interrupted you.
> *Estragon:* On the contrary.
> > *They glare at each other angrily.*
> *Vladimir:* Ceremonious ape!
> *Estragon:* Punctilious pig!
> *Vladimir:* Finish your phrase, I tell you!
> *Estragon:* Finish your own! (pp. 48–48A)]

Here again, as in the case of games, language is used in an empty
and meaningless manner with no real desire to communicate. Furthermore, this politeness serves as a mask for the growing irritation
of both men called for in the stage directions.

The hybrid language of the bums clouds their identity as much
as their several names, their lack of association with any specific
geographical location, etc. Vladimir, for example, has recourse to
baby talk (as in his lullaby), and while he uses a great deal of slang
he also falls back on pompous platitudes and Latin quotations. Estragon, who uses baby talk on more than one occasion in this brief
play, also makes rather frequent use of crude speech and, in general, has a lower level of speech than Vladimir—yet he claims to

be a poet! This discrepancy between the speech of Vladimir and
that of Estragon reenforces the previously established idea that
Vladimir is the more rationally inclined; Estragon, the more emotive.
The social alienation of Estragon and Vladimir is carried out in
a linguistic alienation hinted at when Pozzo uses "knouk" (pp. 38,
39), a word not in the vocabulary of Estragon and Vladimir.

Thus, certain societal phenomena appear through the language
of the play; just as disintegration and mock integration are mirrored
in the speech of the characters so also are *"social"* disintegration
and mock integration. This can be seen in the pronoun shifts of *te,*
nous, me (p. 68), which show social disintegration contrasting with
mock integration as reflected in the pronoun shifts in the passage
following:

Vladimir: Toi aussi, tu dois être content, au fond, avoue-le.
Estragon: Content de quoi?
Vladimir: De m'avoir retrouvé.
Estragon: Tu crois?
Vladimir: Dis-le, même si ce n'est pas vrai.
Estragon: Qu'est-ce que je dois dire?
Vladimir: Dis, Je suis content.
Estragon: Je suis content.
Vladimir: Moi aussi.
Estragon: Moi aussi.
Vladimir: Nous sommes contents.
Estragon: Nous sommes contents. *(Silence.)* Qu'est-ce qu'on fait,
    maintenant qu'on est content?
Vladimir: On attend Godot.
Estragon: C'est vrai. (p. 69)

[*Vladimir:* You must be happy too, deep down, if you only knew it.
Estragon: Happy about what?
Vladimir: To be back with me again.
Estragon: Would you say so?
Vladimir: Say you are, even if it's not true.
Estragon: What am I to say?
Vladimir: Say, I am happy.
Estragon: I am happy.
Vladimir: So am I.
Estragon: So am I.

Vladimir: We are happy.
Estragon: We are happy. *(Silence.)* What do we do now, now that
we are happy?
Vladimir: Wait for Godot. *(Estragon groans. Silence.)* (pp. 38A–39)]

This passage, though predominantly another parrotlike language
game in the same category as the vaudeville routines, nevertheless
shows an effort towards social integration.

The play's hollow sound effects support the themes of horror and
of conversational emptiness. Staccato sound repetitions occur in
such phrases as "Dis, Didi" (p. 18) and in Vladimir's lullaby, which
is comprised of the words "Do do do do" repeated over and over.
Empty resonances also are found in the names Godin, Godet, Godot uttered by Pozzo. These names resound in turn against Estragon's nickname Gogo. The plosive sounds and the abruptness of the
alliterative monosyllables "Pense, porc" (pp. 50–51) applied to
Lucky heighten the sense of the dehumanizing processes present
in the language and are far more effective in doing this than "Pense,
cochon" would be, for example. The rhymes, the alliterations, the
assonances of the vaudeville routines effect their tempo, giving a
sense of rapidity and invention. ("Ces ossements/Evidemment/
. . . commencement" [p. 74], or "Un délassement/Une distraction/
Un délassement" [p. 79], or again "Une illusion/Une hallucination/
Une illusion" [p. 101].)[14]
These hollow sounds, together with the language games and the
monologues, are in sharp contrast to the periods of silence that re-
cur throughout the play. These silences function on several levels,
ranging from the social to the metaphysical. Silence serves to express moral indignation, as when Vladimir refuses to speak to Pozzo
because of Pozzo's treatment of Lucky. His attempt at ostracism
through silence is not very successful, however, and his curiosity
is kindled by mention of Godot, so he is almost forced to speak
despite himself (p. 33). At an intermediate level, silence marks the
momentary exhaustion of subject matter (a period for refueling). It
is invoked by Vladimir, who when the chatter becomes unbearable
suggests that they stop talking for a little while (p. 17).
The tension between sound and silence,[15] which appears at the
beginning of the play and becomes more pronounced by the end,

reflects two basic and paradoxical aspects of man's metaphysical or essential nature—his compulsion to speak, which is social, and his condemnation to silence, which is a manifestation of his solitude. This paradox is achieved by juxtaposing Lucky's muteness to the incessant chatter of Estragon and Vladimir, and it is further demonstrated by Vladimir's and Estragon's periods of alternating silence and conversation. As the "dialogue" of the play shows, language is a faulty mirror of reality, and, furthermore, our use of language reflects egocentricity. Therefore, we fail to communicate; our use of language seems to become more and more trivial. Beckett appears to be saying that since language is used in the manner of the characters of *En attendant Godot* we might do better to choose the other side of the paradox, condemnation to silence. Thus, communication through silence and gesture as in the pantomime is just as effective and perhaps more so than communication through the spoken word. Yet, to silence oneself[16] is to cease to perform the activities that are the most social and the most human and is, in a sense, to die, perhaps not so much in a negative sense as in a positive, a mystical sense: to die out of the world and to erase the contamination that civilization carries along with it.[17]

This yearning for silence in Beckett can be associated with the yearning for silence in Wittgenstein and Heidegger. Both philosophers elaborate a theory of speech that compels them to be silent about the very tasks that they have undertaken. Wittgenstein, whose analysis of language in the *Tractatus* culminates in a vision or silent intuition of logical form, further reenforces silence in his later writings, where he confines philosophic activity to the analysis of ordinary language or language in use. His reduction of speech to ordinary language allows him to say nothing about the foundations of speech or the natural order of the world. Heidegger, on the other hand, focuses his attention on ontology but finds himself able to speak only of historicity. He can say nothing of the principles that underlie the world in process. Both philosophers, therefore, are reduced to the activity of analyzing what the case is (the chatter of Estragon and Vladimir). They must remain silent about the principles that underlie their analysis (the nature of Godot, for example). As Stanley Rosen demonstrates, the choice of silence is the choice some make when faced with the failure of speech.[18] This is the choice of the nihilist.

5

WAITING FOR DEATH

The pivotal theme of *En attendant Godot* is death, man's ultimate limitation. Life, as portrayed in this play, is bleak, sterile, meaningless; and the height of its absurdity, its purposelessness, is shown implicitly by the existence of literal, physical death. The characters refuse to face this fact head-on and only rarely are glimmers of this truth found in their conversations. All of their waiting is a waiting for death, all of their activities are a would-be postponement of death. The subject of death flits in and out of their conversation with no more effect upon them than any other topic. They trifle with the notion of death by contemplating suicide, as if it were merely another game to erase the tedium of life. Likewise, homicide is alluded to as a means of ridding oneself of an obstacle in the form of another human being.

But no decision is ever reached, no action is performed, in terms of these intimations. The one thing that is clear to Beckett's characters is that life, however barren or painful, is preferable to death. Their broken-down moral codes are mere remnants of civilization, ineffective in coping with the nothingness their existence represents. Happiness, a supposed outcome of moral codes, is for these men a mirage in the desert of their lives. The pessimism inherent in this view of things is compounded by the fact that the lives of these men are meant to stand for the lives of *all* men; for all men, in Beckett's view, seek to evade death by maneuvers that are ultimately absurd. This absurdity has its origins in man's lack of clear-cut freedom. He is imprisoned within himself and so cannot transcend the limitations of the tools that he must use to live (his body, mind, and memory), nor can he communicate with others. It is devastating to realize, too, that man may be imprisoned by his own myth-making tendencies, a notion barely perceived by any of the characters in the play, although Vladimir appears to get certain intimations of this during and after his conversations with the messenger boy.

The aimlessness of the life led by Vladimir and Estragon, and even by Pozzo and Lucky, though preferable to death, will come to an end only with death, after which there will be nothing. In our opinion, there is no other way to read this play.

An indication that death is the basic theme of *En attendant Godot* is that death is alluded to no less than five times in the first seven pages of dialogue,[1] and a great many scattered references to death occur throughout the play, including allusions to homicide and suicide. But further proof of this thesis is that four old men in the twilight of life are waiting either for salvation from their predicament or for the night, which is clearly symbolic of death.[2] They can be viewed as being at different stages of declension, with Lucky appearing to be the closest to death.[3] Furthermore, their environment is a wasteland in which a single tree (in Act I without leaves) is growing. The audience, also part of the environment of the characters, is construed to be a bog in Act I (p. 16); but in Act II it is viewed by Estragon and Vladimir as a charnel house, full of bones and cadavers (p. 74). Thus, the audience represents something to be avoided, because, as is the case with any structured society, it engulfs and deadens the individual. Furthermore, the effect of the passage in Act II is to suggest that all of humanity is in death's toils, not just the characters. This passage, like the names of the characters, is a means of universalizing the substance of the play.

Death is a subject that figures frequently, either in a veiled or an overt manner, in the characters' conversation. The hidden allusions are often couched in the metaphor of night, which lends itself readily to notions of sleep (that state of man most nearly akin to death) and of fearful darkness. This subconscious awareness of the analogy between night and death, though occurring innumerable times in the play, is best shown in the passage already cited in which Pozzo describes the rapidity with which night (old age and

death) descends upon man (Fr., p. 88; Eng., p. 99). Estragon and
Vladimir respond to this soliloquy by saying that as long as they are
forewarned and know what to "expect" they have only to "wait."
This response carries with it the implicit idea that man is waiting
for more than (or at times something other than) Godot—for the
night, that is, and, though he may not say so in so many words, for
death. Such is very possibly the implication of Vladimir's faltering,
perhaps even incomplete, statement, "Nous ne sommes plus seuls,
à attendre la nuit, à attendre Godot, à attendre—à attendre" (p. 88)
["We are no longer alone, waiting for the night, waiting for Godot,
waiting for . . . waiting. All evening we have struggled, unassisted.
Now it's over. It's already to-morrow" (p. 50)]. So terrible is the
third alternative that Vladimir cannot verbalize it. Indeed, until the
final moments of this play overt reference to death in any *serious*
context is largely avoided. Pozzo, in his final pronouncement on
time, enunciates the theme of death (and its connection with the
night) unequivocally when he says: " . . . un jour nous sommes nés,
un jour nous mourrons, le même jour, le même instant, ça ne vous
suffit pas? . . . Elles accouchent à cheval sur une tombe, le jour
brille un instant, puis c'est la nuit à nouveau" (p. 104) [". . . one
day we were born, one day we shall die, the same day, the same
second, is that not enough for you? . . . They give birth astride of
a grave, the light gleams an instant, then it's night once more" (p.
57A)]. Vladimir picks up and develops this theme in his final monologue, saying:"A cheval sur une tombe et une naissance difficile.
Du fond du trou, rêveusement, le fossoyeur applique ses fers. On
a le temps de vieillir. L'air est plein de nos cris" (pp. 105–06)
["Astride of a grave and a difficult birth. Down in the hole, lingeringly, the gravedigger puts on the forceps. We have time to grow
old. The air is full of our cries" (pp. 58–58A)].

Up to this point overt reference to death had been largely to homicide (as a means of ridding oneself of a nuisance) and to suicide
(mostly as a new kind of game). Marissel in his study on Beckett
has rightly observed that each person has at least one hangman and
one victim.[4] If Lucky is Pozzo's victim in Act I, Pozzo can be considered Lucky's victim in Act II, for Lucky is the potential leader
and has the real advantage over the blind Pozzo—if he wishes to
use this advantage.[5] Similarly, Estragon is sometimes Vladimir's

hangman (when he challenges Vladimir's reason, thus his life-style) and sometimes Vladimir's victim (Vladimir calls most of the shots; it is his idea to wait for Godot). The hangman/victim motif occurs in various forms in the play, under the guise of the masochist/sadist, master/slave combinations, in the form of the allusions to Cain and Abel (p. 96) and to the crucifixion (pp. 13, 62). If man strives to avoid his own death, he often wishes it or seeks it for others, especially when they are in his way, as is seen not only in the preceding cases but also when Pozzo maintains that the only way to get rid of beings like Lucky is to have them killed (p. 37). By no means a coincidence, the words in the round that Vladimir sings echo all the themes of the Lucky/Pozzo relationship (masochism/sadism, brutality, death, even murder). At another point in the play (p. 71), Estragon remarks that if Vladimir finds him to be a burden, he can kill him. He further hints that Vladimir has had recourse to murder at some point in the past, and when Vladimir demands clarification ("Quel autre?"), Estragon becomes evasive: "Comme des billions d'autres" (p. 71).

> [*Estragon:* The best thing would be to kill me, like the other.
> *Vladimir:* What other? *(Pause.)* What other?
> *Estragon:* Like billions of others. (p. 40)]

Despite the ambiguity of this reply, there are undeniable hints of genocide in it. Furthermore, to be a witness of death as well as its agent and victim suggests the plight of every man and is one of the bases for tragedy—if indeed *En attendant Godot* is a tragedy.

One can, of course, be one's own hangman and one's own victim,[6] and this is potentially the situation of Vladimir and Estragon, as the play's five separate references to suicide strongly suggest. In three of these references the instruments of death, whether man-made or natural, are not considered sufficient. The branch of the tree is thought to be too weak; the cord holding up Estragon's trousers is not strong enough either. When the instruments of suicide are adequate (the Eiffel Tower, the Durance), either the will is not there or a conflict of wills interrupts the act. These are, of course, examples of the *suicide raté* found in the traditional mime.[7]

The theme of suicide in *En attendant Godot* has interesting variations. Estragon once attempted to commit suicide by throwing himself in the Durance, an attempt that was frustrated by Vladimir, who came to his rescue (p. 63). This instance of suicide is, of course, tied to the salvation theme of the play, with Vladimir functioning again as the father figure. In the context of the play the implication of this episode seems to be that salvation can occur with any degree of certainty only on physical and social levels. Vladimir's "salvation" of Estragon is charged with irony, for he saved Estragon for nothing but a life of misery, a "chaudepisse d'existence . . . dans la Merdecluse" (p. 71). (In the English version of the play he says he is in a muckheap. The French is vulgar and plays on the place name Vaucluse.)

An additional irony is that, although Vladimir has saved Estragon from suicide in the past, he nevertheless maintains that they should have committed suicide by throwing themselves off the Eiffel Tower, "an eternity ago, in about 1900" (p. 10). Vladimir's commentary at this point suggests that suicide is meaningful only when one is young, not so much for the number of years of life given up—since that is unknown—but because one is not yet waiting for death, nor is one yet ready to compromise. He appears to think that it is now too late.

But even though suicide has meaning only for the young (or so Vladimir seems to suggest), thoughts of suicide, like thoughts of other manners of dying, can be toyed with; but in any real sense it must be postponed. In the course of the play suicide is discussed three times as a way of eliminating ennui and is each time rejected. These discussions occur at points where other games have momentarily been exhausted and thus take on the form of a proposal for a new kind of game (pp. 19, 62–63, 108–109).

Although in Act II Vladimir maintains that they almost hanged themselves on the tree that Estragon does not remember (p. 70), this is not exactly true, for suicide is never seriously contemplated at this point in their existence. However great their despair, they prefer life to death.[8] Despite Brick's suggestion that the reason one does not commit suicide at all is that one continues to exist for one's partner's sake,[9] we believe that this is merely an excuse on the part of Estragon, and at that it is only one excuse among many for not taking one's life (they are too old; the branch is too weak; the cord breaks). The real reason that they cannot commit suicide is that man is condemned to live; he must "continue,"[10] as Vladimir himself recognizes: "Je ne peux pas continuer. *Un temps.* Qu'est-ce que j'ai dit" (p. 106) ["I can't go on! *(Pause.)* What have I said?" (p. 58A)]. The prospect of death is more terrible than the prospect of continuing to confront the tedium and despair of existence. If life as here depicted by Beckett is absurd, the attempt to escape it by suicide can be even more absurd, as is shown in the final moments of the play, when Estragon, who has removed the cord holding up his trousers with the intention of using it to hang himself and Vladimir, is told to pull up his trousers, which are ludicrously down around his feet. Thus the characters, even Lucky, prefer to wait for death rather than escape the hell of existence by the only effective means available—that of suicide.

Life, no matter how imperfectly known, is to be preferred to death, about which even less is known. Furthermore, the play promotes the conclusion that no theology really frees man from his desire to escape physical death. All else is speculation and is therefore subject to the utmost skepticism.

Yet the play does suggest that human beings need something to believe in—some myth, some hero to give the illusion of order or of continuity, as well as a sense of outside purpose. So strong is this need to believe, that it exists concomitantly with doubt in that very belief. Vladimir, though virtually certain that Godot will not come tomorrow, nevertheless tells Estragon that they will wait for Godot again tomorrow evening.

Even so, within the world of the play negativism prevails.[11] No myth will work, for Beckett allows only pejorative meanings of this word. Nothing actually improves man's finite situation.

The theology of *En attendant Godot* is deliberately confused. It appears to reflect modern occidental man's eclectic theology with all its paradoxes. Vladimir and Estragon are striving to replace a crumbling Christian theology with a belief in a supposed reality existing in the here and now. They hold no apparent belief in an afterlife or in the Parousia; for them salvation is in the coming of Godot. At times they seem to believe in the conventional Christian god, perhaps reflecting habits of thought or influence from their

cultural or linguistic environment. Furthermore, they do not con-
fuse God with Godot, as can be seen in Estragon's wondering
whether God sees him (p. 87) and in his ejaculation that God have
pity on him (p. 88). He does not wonder if Godot sees him; he does
not pray that Godot have pity on him. In addition, Vladimir, upon
hearing that Godot has a white beard exclaims "Miséricorde" (p.
107) ["Christ have mercy on us!" (p. 59A)]. This exclamation, which
can be explained as a mere linguistic habit, nevertheless, coming
as it does at this moment of stress, shows vestiges of Christian upbringing or of a Christian orientation.[12] Estragon purports to emulate Jesus by going barefoot (p. 62); no character seeks to emulate
the virtually unknown Godot. But to add to the irony, Estragon has
demonstrated a very hazy notion of Christ, whom he does not recognize when He is referred to as the Saviour (p. 13). While Vladimir's and Estragon's concepts of sin and repentance (which are,
incidentally, very vague) are also based on the ruins of Christianity,
they are not dependent in any way on Godot. However, Vladimir
and Estragon do ascribe the notion of a punishing God to Godot
(p. 108). Perhaps this fusion occurs because of the allusions to sheep
and goats in the conversations with the messenger boy(s), despite
the ironic reversal in which it is the sheepherder who is beaten.[13]
But such allusions to Christianity are not to be taken seriously.
These men have no more hope in the Christian God than they do
in Godot (p. 24).

  As a matter of fact, the play can quite readily be construed as an
anti-Christian play. The tree, which many critics have viewed as a
symbol of the cross, may be taken at face value as a symbol of nature, in which case its flourishing in the midst of human decay and
chaos signifies that nature is impervious to man. If, on the other
hand, the tree is interpreted as a sign of the cross,[14] it is significant,
first of all, that Vladimir and Estragon are incapable of recognizing
it even as a tree, much less as a symbol of their resurrection. The
tree is, of course, the signpost of their earthly rendezvous and sub-
sequent salvation, but they are not in the least sure that it is the
right tree, or, as we have just said, that it is even a tree. Furthermore, the tree is for them a potential instrument of death (a
means of suicide, which is scarcely Christian) and not the means to
everlasting life. Finally, the conversation at the beginning of the

play concerning the two thieves, in which Vladimir states that in one of the Gospels the Saviour did not want to save the two thieves from death (p. 14), not only introduces the "salvation" theme, but, more importantly, stresses the theme of man's overriding desire to escape physical death, which must, in strictest terms, be considered unchristian. The entire problem of a God who is so cruel as to permit such evils as man's physical death (as if to suggest that his life on earth were his paradise, his purgatory, and his hell) is evoked by this allusion. Still, the relative cruelty or kindness of God is not a (and certainly not *the*) subject of the play, chiefly because God is not a subject, unless in a negative sense. In the world of *En attendant Godot* God does not exist, or if He does exist He is indifferent to man: the aphasia and apathy of God referred to in Lucky's speech are evidence of this. Thus, if one insists on identifying the tree as the cross (as we do not), then man before Christ (Act I) is no better off than man after Christ (Act II, following the flowering of the "cross").[15] Indeed, if Lucky's speech is examined carefully man appears to be worse off, for he is in the constant process of shrinking, intellectually, physically, and spiritually. This is the very epitome of an anti-Christian world view.

The remnants of Christian theology in the conversations of Vladimir and Estragon contrast with the attitudes of Pozzo and Lucky that contribute to the agnostic tone of the play. That Pozzo is a fatalist, perhaps an atheist, is evident from his statement that the roles he and Lucky fulfill are a matter of chance (p. 36). As can be the case with a certain type of atheist, he has set himself up as a kind of god. By his own testimony he is of divine origin (p. 26) and cannot be made to suffer (p. 40), and he deals out punishments and rewards in an authoritarian manner. Although he shows signs of having what might be called a Christian conscience, it is a superficial one at best,[16] and the self-centered value system in terms of which he behaves most of the time is quite alien to a Christian code. Lucky's acceptance of Pozzo's tyranny, on the other hand, constitutes an endorsement of Pozzo's life-style. In a very special sense, Pozzo is Lucky's hero, an earthly replacement of the Christian God, analogous to what Godot is to Vladimir and Estragon.

The morality of the characters in the play is as deliberately confused as their theology.[17] Vladimir appears to embody the three

theological virtues of faith, hope, and charity: it is he who insists
repeatedly upon waiting for Godot, continues to hope despite his
subconscious despair (pp. 107–08), is shocked by Pozzo's treatment
of Lucky (p. 32). But none of these virtues, especially that of charity,
is deep-seated. His sympathy for Lucky (p. 32) is quickly transferred
to Pozzo by Pozzo's maneuvering of Vladimir's indignation (p. 39).
That neither Vladimir nor Estragon is really moved by Pozzo's
shocking abuse of Lucky is further indicated by their remarks immediately after the exit of Pozzo and Lucky; the episode has helped
Vladimir and Estragon pass the time that day (p. 57). Vladimir's
Christian morality never really leads to action. In his exhortation
concerning humanitarian acts (p. 91), counterarguments can be detected ("Ce n'est pas qu'on ait précisément besoin de nous")[18] that
serve to postpone and ultimately to preclude action.[19] When Vladimir and Estragon finally do give assistance to Pozzo, they act not
out of any moral consideration but in the mere "course of events."
In short, Vladimir's morality is a hodgepodge, based in part on certain reflexes growing out of a Christian humanism no more clearly
thought out or defined than his theology. Estragon, an egocentric
hedonist, has even fewer vestiges of Christian morality than Vladimir. His one charitable act, that of leaving his shoes for another,
has in reality a selfish motivation—the shoes hurt his feet. He con-
templates good deeds only when he suspects that they may benefit
him materially and is so petty that he hopes for Lucky's death as
a fitting punishment for Lucky's having kicked him, a desire for
vengeance that runs counter to Christian morality. Vladimir does
not try to dissuade Estragon and, indeed, points out to him that
should Estragon need to beat Lucky in order to rouse him it will
be an opportunity for vengeance (p. 101). Finally, Estragon's pseudo-
Christian charity is not only contradicted by these vengeful desires,
but also by the selfishness he manifests when he insists that God
have pity on *him* (p. 88), his pleasure in witnessing Vladimir's pain
(pp. 40–41), and his assertion that helping others gets one into a
mess (p. 95). Selfishness and materialism are more dominant in
Estragon than are any positive moral traits.

The unchristian tendencies present in Estragon and Vladimir are
even more pronounced in Pozzo, who has the wealth and the power
to force his will upon others. He is a type of superman whose values

do not emanate from a social order; rather, the order emanates from him. He has very little respect for the human being and accepts Vladimir and Estragon only because they are useful to him. The utilitarian approach is most conspicuous in his inhumane treatment of Lucky. Lucky—the machine—must not break down, for if he were to become ill, it would be a grave inconvenience for Pozzo (p. 31). Lucky's passive, even abject acceptance of Pozzo's value system represents an abdication of his human rights as well as a dismissal of his own moral position, whatever that may have been. His total submission to Pozzo is carried to the absurd when in Act II he continues to tote the baggage for the now blind Pozzo, especially since it contains nothing but sand.

Thus, *En attendant Godot* contains a mixed morality. In Vladimir and Estragon a disintegrating Christian morality is in the process of being replaced by an egocentric one. In Pozzo, whatever Christian morality there may have been has vanished utterly and the individual reigns supreme, having no regard for the other man's rights, and yet this supremacy is not challenged. Beckett does not seem to be endorsing one code or criticizing the other. He seems to be saying, rather, that man's ability to evolve an effective moral code is limited by his finitude and, in this case, primarily by his egocentric nature, which comes into conflict with his occasional desire to be altruistic.

The ambiguous morality of the characters affects their hazy concept of happiness. Apparently, happiness can be apprehended solely by negatives. Only Estragon actually says that he is unhappy (p. 59). It is easy for him to do so: his feet hurt, he is tired, he is bored. Lucky also knows when he is unhappy and shows his unhappiness by weeping. His "happiness" is derived from Pozzo's sadistic treatment, his unhappiness from the idea of separation from Pozzo when that becomes imminent (p. 37). Conversely, Vladimir and the messenger boy do not know whether they are happy or unhappy (p. 61). Vladimir's uncertainty is tied to his rationality, which makes for a confused morality and is, furthermore, a strong indication that he does not expect Godot to arrive, because from a technical point of view the degree to which one has attained one's goal determines the degree to which one is happy or unhappy. However, Vladimir's values are so muddled that it is doubtful if he would know whether he were happy or not, even if Godot arrived. Although Vladimir has leanings toward rationalism, he is a skeptic; he can endorse neither bodily pleasures nor mental pursuits strongly enough to achieve the happiness that might come from one or the other.

That happiness is a difficult state to achieve or sustain is shown in three somewhat different ways: as a past condition not to be recovered, a fantasy to be dreamed about and never attained, or as a state to be sought after in the world of make-believe. Pozzo, untroubled in Act I, speaks nostalgically in Act II of the time when he had his sight and evokes from Vladimir the comment that remembered happiness must be painful (p. 99). Ironically, by the absence of the faculty, its presence comes to be associated with happiness. Significantly, Vladimir and not Pozzo regards Pozzo's sighted past as having been happy. Estragon, toward the end of the play, is distressed because Vladimir has awakened him at a moment when he was dreaming of being happy. Unfortunately, he says nothing about what he construes happiness to be. Finally, Vladimir and Estragon devise a linguistic game in which they *tell* each other that they are happy, as if to imply that repeating the word "content" often enough will actually bring about a state of contentment. In other words they are deluding themselves into thinking that habit will induce happiness, that happiness can be brought about artificially.

Here again the implication is that finite man cannot achieve real or lasting happiness, partially because he discovers that his various concepts of happiness do not prove out, partially because of his confused theology or his confused sense of morality, partially because man may not recognize happiness until it has passed away, assuming that it ever existed. Life is a purgatory in which happiness may not exist except through the total negation of everything—through absolute silence, absolute immobility—a negation only achievable, if at all, through physical death.[20]

Because of the confused picture of theology and morality presented by Beckett's characters, no clear concept of human freedom emerges from the play. To the extent that there is such a thing as freedom in Beckett's view, it appears in the play on the social and metaphysical planes: the social through Pozzo and Lucky, the metaphysical through Vladimir and Estragon. Lucky's being tied literally and figuratively to Pozzo and Pozzo's fatalism render the argument for their freedom somewhat tenuous. Pozzo operates as if he were self-determined and self-determining; however, he recognizes that he is what he is only because of Lucky, and he is also dependent upon Vladimir and Estragon. The case of Lucky is fraught with problems. It is unclear, for one thing, whether he is Pozzo's slave by choice or by chance, and although in Act II he seemingly could free himself from the blind Pozzo, he is by then unable to end their relationship. The situation of Vladimir and Estragon is similarly ambivalent, on the metaphysical level. Estragon is concerned about the degree of freedom they have, as is seen in his asking repeatedly whether or not they are tied to Godot. Vladimir ultimately answers emphatically that they are not tied to Godot ("jamais de la vie"), but he pauses after this strong statement and then adds a highly significant "not yet" ("pas encore" [p. 24]). This assertion on Vladimir's part is explicitly contradicted by Vladimir himself when he tells Estragon that they have sold out their rights (suggesting that once they were free, p. 21), as well as by the whole course of the play: that they are tied to Godot is evident in their inability to cease their waiting for him even when everything indicates that he will never come. Vladimir's one assertion concerning the will ("vouloir, tout est là" [p. 97]) [Simple question of will-power (p. 54)] is every bit as ironic as their pointless waiting, for at no time are the wills of Estragon and Vladimir operative. On the contrary, they are as much enslaved by a whole bundle of habits as Pozzo and Lucky are. And this habit-ridden existence carries with it a postponement, indeed an evasion of any choice that might alleviate the ennui and anxiety that oppress them.[21] If such a thing as the "will" does exist[22]—in Beckett's view it may not—then it is atrophied in Vladimir and Estragon, and in Lucky and Pozzo as well, at least by the end of the play. And the cause of this atrophy is habit "the great deadener" ("la grande sourdine"). The foregoing discussion implies that the characters of *En attendant Godot* do not have a sense of responsibility, though on the surface certain remarks suggest that perhaps they do. While Pozzo exhibits little or no concern for others, in that he seeks primarily self-gratification, Lucky continues to carry out his duties as porter to the bitter end. This may be interpreted as a sign of Lucky's devotion to Pozzo. On the other hand, perhaps he acts more from habit and fear than out of a sense of responsibility. The friendship between Vladimir and Estragon also seems to carry with it a sense of responsibility: each appears to be concerned about the welfare of the other, Vladimir perhaps more than Estragon. But the ambivalence and the habitual nature of their relationship are the real explanations of their seeming concern for one another.

Critics often point out Vladimir's "nous ne sommes pas des saints, mais nous sommes au rendez-vous" (p. 91) [We are not saints, but have kept our appointment (p. 51B)] as a mark of virtue, especially the virtue of constancy (which is closely akin to a sense of responsibility).[23] Yet, since the keeping of the appointment is always fruitless, it seems a bit far of the mark to call this a virtue or even to make much of a point of it. Once again this is a case of habitual activity.

Thus, although the characters do express concern, their concern is not genuine, and this lack of a true sense of responsibility only magnifies the solitude of each of the characters, who are not really concerned with others but are, rather, preoccupied with their own egos. This manifestly is not the Sartrian concept of freedom and responsibility, but instead a notion of man's imprisonment through habit and egoism, which prevents him from acting in any truly meaningful or purposeful manner.

Indeed, throughout the play evidence is found of egoistical solipsism—in the characters' value systems (or morality), in their failure to communicate, in their dealings with one another. The other two forms of solipsism, the epistemological and metaphysical forms, are not explicitly in evidence since the characters do not even discuss either the self as the source of existential knowledge or the self as being all that exists. Implicitly, however, considering the egoism of the characters, the suggestion is that everyone is confined to his own experience and thus can know only himself and his own experiences, and this leads to the conclusion that existence for these characters, in Beckett's view, revolves around the self. Therefore it can be said that traces of metaphysical and epistemological solipsism are present in the play. Yet, all three forms of solipsism presuppose a concept of self, and, since the concept of the self as it pertains to identity is questionable in Beckett, some doubt arises whether there is any real solipsism present in *Godot*. This is another ramification of the skepticism, already discussed, wherein the self, being made up of many individuals, cannot be known, partially because it does not exist in the conventional sense of the word (that is, as a unity). Hence, in *En attendant Godot* the characters seem to demonstrate some sort of pluralistic solipsism implying the disunity of the self. However, to the extent that evidence of the first form of solipsism is present in the play (egoistical solipsism implying some type of unity), there is a growing egocentricity tending in the direction of absolutes: absolute silence in Lucky, absolute blindness in Pozzo, absolute immobility in Estragon and Vladimir. These absolutes cause the individual to become more and more imprisoned in the purgatory of self, thus magnifying his solitude, for they have the dual effect of cutting the person off from the external world (a source of absurdity of the type designated by Camus)[24] and of forcing him to face what he regards as himself, hence of looking into an abyss.[25]

This solipsism, which has its origins in man's incapacity to transcend himself and, hence, in his finitude, also creates many interrelated paradoxes that in their turn are additional sources of absurdity in *En attendant Godot*. Many of these already have been encountered: man's social nature in conflict with his fundamental solitude; man's dependence and his drive to be independent; man's moral egoism contradicted by his desire to be altruistic; man's dual nature, which is at once rational and affective; man's ambivalence between his drive for love and his equally powerful hostility; man's effort to communicate through speech, frustrated both by the failure of language and by his turning inward toward silence; man's wish to move and to change cancelled out by inertia, habit, etc.

Further absurdity arises from man's difficulty in identifying reality, that is, in distinguishing between night and day, sleeping and waking, life and death, etc.

Absurdity also can be noted in the ennui and repetitiveness that characterize the existence of man as he is portrayed in this play. Like Sisyphus pushing the rock up the hill over and over again, Lucky continues to carry the baggage when it contains nothing but sand, and each evening Vladimir and Estragon renew their hopeless waiting for Godot. And indeed the greatest absurdity of all is the subconscious effort of the characters to transend self, time, and more importantly death through a non-existent God (Godot?). And all of this is true of man's condition as it seems to us to be portrayed in *En attendant Godot*, notwithstanding Beckett's own statement that his work is not about the absurd condition of man.[26]

This absurdity creates a feeling of hopelessness, for there is reason to believe that the characters subconsciously apprehend the exhausting emptiness and triviality of their existence. Such sentences as "I'm unhappy," "Will night never come," "I'm tired," bear witness to this. Furthermore, this particular hopelessness, which is nihilistic in effect, reenforces by its lack of faith in values outside the self the selfishness and callousness of the characters, so that the matter of egoism comes full circle.

There can be little question that Beckett's world view in *En attendant Godot* is nihilistic since the play revolves around a fundamental disbelief in man as he is and as he probably would continue to be under any circumstance: finite, petty, and with no ultimate purposes. This negative view is incorporated into the very structure of the written play: it begins with the negative word "nothing" and ends with the equally negative sentence "They do not move." When enacted, the play opens on a negative note with the sentence "nothing to be done" and ends on a negative note with the nonarrival of Godot and the nondeparture of Vladimir and Estragon. Indeed, the negativism is so strong that the absolutes just discussed (absolute silence, absolute inertia), which would normally be considered imperfections, appear here to be ideal states, comparable to the nihilistic yearning for silence that Wittgenstein, due to his recognition of the limitations of language and reason, expresses in his *Tractatus* and also to notions of silence found in Heidegger.[27] These absolutes represent, in fact, the only way outside of death of overcoming the paradoxes of human existence. Such a nihilistic view makes the argument that *En attendant Godot* is a Christian morality play patently inadmissible. We must also disagree with those critics who think it possible to find an ultimate optimism in the play.[28] We agree instead with G. E. Wellworth, who finds total pessimism in the work of Beckett.[29] And, although Lucky's monologue suggests that man has retrogressed, in Beckett's view man never has and never will overcome his finitude: he is a victim of his own nature, lacking the dignity and solidarity that Camus has seen as a means of contending with the absurdity of life. Far from banding together to fight those evils that are death-producing, the characters of *En attendant Godot* refuse almost deliberately to even recognize death, the thought of which would be salutary in the Pascalian view, but is here avoided, in part because it spells out the end of the ego. Although death is staring Vladimir and Estragon in the face, they indulge in trivial pastimes destined to divert their attention from what they are really waiting for—not the arrival of Godot, but of death. It seems to us that Beckett is criticizing this attitude, for, even though death means an inevitable nothingness, it would be one of quite a different order from the nothingness of existence[30] and should furthermore be desirable since it constitutes a sure cure for the tragedy of birth. This nihilistic pessimism of Beckett obviates classifying him among twentieth-century humanists such as Sartre and Camus. To quote the terse statement of Huguette Delye, "Now, Beckett does not like Man."[31]

If, then, Beckett takes such a dismal view of man's endeavors, what is his view of man as it emerges in this play? Is man a clown or is he a tragic hero? In other words, is the play a comedy, a tragedy, or a tragicomedy? Or is the play what some contemporary critics call an antiplay? Finally, having the view he appears to have, why does Beckett write? How does he conceive the role of the artist? What for him is the function of art? The following chapter attempts to resolve these important aesthetic issues.

6

TRAGEDY OR COMEDY

William Thompson, discussing the "drama of the absurd" in his article "Freedom and Comedy," describes the mask that the "absurd hero" asumes. "Half the audience," he writes, "will see the mask as tragic; half the audience will see the mask as comic. The audience will be right, for the human condition does not change; we have the same ancient choice: we can laugh or we can cry."[1] It is quite true that critics as well as audiences are divided in their reaction to *En attendant Godot*. Yet there is good reason to argue that the characters in the play belong neither to comedy nor to tragedy, at which we choose to laugh or else to cry, but to a subtle fusion of the two modes. The play may very well be a "tragicomedy in two acts," as Beckett himself calls it in the English edition, though it is surely not a conventional tragicomedy, if we mean by this a play having tragic tone and tragic peripetia but normally having a *dénouement* plunged into a probably happy future. The superficial comedy of the play, which makes us laugh at first, is abruptly interrupted by our sudden recognition of the potential tragedy in the human situation as it is portrayed here. However, there is every possibility that a deeper level of comedy lies beneath the apparent tragedy, and that we are being called upon to laugh, perhaps unwittingly, at things we would not ordinarily consider laughable. What may be appropriate here is the dianoetic laughter—the mirthless, sardonic laugh—that Beckett describes in *Watt*.[2] This, of course, is the laughter that comes with the recognition of an absurdity that overrides the tragedy in the human condition. In other words, it is not so much a question of whether *En attendant Godot* is a tragedy or a comedy but rather whether a unilateral response to it is or is not appropriate. We, the audience, may not readily make the third step that would complete the cycle of responses from comedy to tragedy to comedy, but it seems likely that Beckett himself has made the necessary transitions. He may then laugh not only at the characters in his play but at the "tears" in the audience. If then, Beckett views a tragic plight with which we tend to sympathize as ultimately comic, his opinion of man is indeed as pessimistic as we have been contending that it is and raises the question as to what his artistic ends may be. Again conventional answers, such as "catharsis," punishment through ridicule, and so forth, are unacceptable. Beckett's aesthetic viewpoint can be discerned to some extent in the play itself. We find evidence here (as in his other writings) that art may constitute a diversion, however momentary, from the tedium of existence. If this is the case, then art may be nothing more than a meaningless game, and Beckett may be as much against it as for it.

The aspect of comedy in *En attendant Godot* that one may call superficial is conventional in nature, having its origins in the farce, the *commedia dell'arte*, and pantomimic and vaudevillian traditions. Comic devices belonging in this category have already been noted in the course of this study but may be conveniently recapitulated at this point. Physical comedy, for example, is found in such things as falling and stumbling, and in the voyeurism of Estragon. On a somewhat higher level, we have linguistic comedy coming from repetitions, puns, misunderstandings, scatalogical word play and from ceremonial and ritualistic uses of language.[3] From vaudeville we have the linguistic routines, the hat exchange, the fallen pants, the unzipped fly, the general outlandish clothing of the characters, including their derbies. Aborted suicides (due to broken ropes and the like) come from the pantomime; and *commedia dell'arte* as well as pantomime give us the stock farcical characters, certainly the clowns, or *zanni*, reflected in Estragon and Vladimir and perhaps even the pedant suggested by Pozzo. Comic effects, that, like certain others listed above, might come from any one of these sources, are achieved through the frequent memory lapses of the characters and through their general failure to communicate.

These effects have in common the fact that they are traditional in comedy, and as a result of this, they automatically evoke laughter in us, as for the most part they also do in the characters. That is to say, though at most times our laughter coincides, there are other times when a matter which is serious for the characters, such as the occasional falls they take or their miscarried efforts to accomplish something, is humorous to us. In almost all of the foregoing, what we are laughing at are human limitations in both the physical and intellectual domains. Such laughter may be termed "social" because, as Bergson notes,[4] we are in agreement concerning the subject for laughter. Our response at this stage is one of detachment. In other words, we are not in sympathy with the scene or situation being portrayed.

In *Godot*, however, the superficial comedy is extended to grotesque exaggerations. These appear in the egotism of the characters, especially the pompousness and platitudinousness of Pozzo, and his mistreatment of Lucky. They can also be observed in the macabre appearance of Lucky, and in the frenzied pace of the games with which Estragon and Vladimir intend to cope with the ever-present ennui. This grotesqueness underlying the superficial comedy is what leads us, correctly or incorrectly, to the tragic mode.

While the characters of the play appear to have no awareness of the grotesqueness and only vague glimmers of the tragic potential of their plight, the audience recognizes both. It would seem at this point, then, that we have a "tragicomedy" of sorts, or in any case a fusion of the tragic and comic modes. This duality in tone finds its echo in the structure of the play, which is built—though not necessarily systematically—on the numerical figure two: there are two acts in the play (can they be said to represent B.C. and A.D.?), two pairs of characters, many two syllable names.[5] The messenger boy has a brother and there is allusion to another set of brothers, Cain and Abel, as well as to the two thieves who were crucified with Jesus. The play-within-a-play adds another dimension to the frame "plot," and this binary construction is also reflected in the presence of both lyrical and rhetorical passages within the one play.[6] Furthermore, this persistent use of twos seems to be another reason for arguing that the play is not a Christian allegory; if it were, its numerical system would probably be three or seven.

The play also reveals itself to be a fusion of tragedy and comedy
through the masks of the various characters. Act I is dominated by
the comic mask Estragon, Act II by the tragic mask Vladimir.[7]
There is an interplay of the two men that intensifies for us the dramatic tension as well as the terribleness of their situation. Reen-
forcing this fusion of genres, in Act I Pozzo wears the comic mask
and Lucky the tragic mask, while in Act II there is a melting of
distinctions between the two characters. We may note here that
Pozzo and Lucky are as antithetical in appearance as they are in
personality and wonder whether the result of this is humor through
contrasts or tragic grotesqueness brought about through dispropor-
tions. In any case, these contrasts heighten our awareness of the
paradoxes having to do with conflicts within man's nature that are
to be found in the play.

The tragic element of *En attendant Godot* does not depend upon
traditional devices, nor can it be called tragic by conventional def-
initions of the word. It has been called an antiplay, on the grounds
that it has no character development and no plot. This lack of plot
or of action is all-important in excluding *Godot* from conventional
tragedy, because insofar as there are no events, there can be no
possibility of an interaction between events and character (no peripetia), no possibility of an outcome (no *noeud,* no *dénouement*) no
tragic recognition, and, despite what Ruby Cohn and others claim,
no transcendence.[8] In addition, we have in this play stylization or
character "types" without any clear identity. There is no development of the characters, no evolution; indeed, if anything, there is
a declension. This, of course, is to be expected, in view of the fact
that these men are victims of their habits and are thus incapable of
voluntary change. In fact, none of the characters can be designated
the tragic hero who "falls" (conventionally, from great heights), and
there is, thus, no sublimity involved. In addition, in this particular
play social condition bears upon the tragic substance in a manner
that is the reverse of the conventional tragedy: it is the man of mean
condition (Lucky) who wears the tragic mask, and the man of rank
and wealth (Pozzo) who wears the comic mask. (However, the distinction is not clear in Act II, in which their roles are blurred.)

We might note that it is not necessary to limit ourselves to ancient
or to seventeenth-century drama in making these contrasts, for even

much prominent twentieth-century tragedy must, unlike *Godot*, be placed within the category of "conventional." This is corroborated by a glance at Montherlant, for example, himself a nihilist, who writes plays that are permeated with Greek ritualistic tragic tone.[9] Similarly, Anouilh presents us with a spectrum of uncompromising rebellious tragic characters (Beckett, l'Alouette, Antigone) who meet catastrophe in a basically conventional manner. In the case of Anouilh, furthermore, we can conclude that his sense of tragedy calls for a type of ensnarement by fate or catastrophe and for a purity of ending allowing for no hope, all of which would render such plays quite Racinian in temperament.[10]

Now, although in *Godot* there is no delving into the individual psychological make-up of the four characters, they are, we have argued, psychological types. Furthermore, as we have also argued, collectively they probably represent universal man. We identify ourselves not with any one character, as we would do with a tragic hero, but rather with the particular situations of the several characters and with the general "human condition." While in the case of the tragic hero we identify with his exceptional and his uncompromising nature, in these four men we recognize another side of ourselves—the side that is all too willing to compromise. The characters of *En attendant Godot* compromise not only with each other but also with their situation, and this is in part why the play can be called an ultramodern tragedy. That is to say, in *En attendant Godot* we do not have a catastrophe or some tragic condition that has been brought about through tragic error; it is man's situation as such, a situation that is neither remediable nor provoked by human manipulation, and that is, therefore, tragic.[11]

The play, then, is a tragedy in the sense that it portrays man as a victim of himself, as a victim of his own finite nature. It is a tragedy portraying the limitations of both reason and imagination. It is deterministic, showing that the will, if it even exists, is limited[12] and yet capable of putting man in a position of willful false optimism if not a willful lack of preoccupation with the tragic elements of his existence. Instead, the characters (who are bound to the realm of forfeiture described by Heidegger in his *Being and Time*) are preoccupied only with trivia: games including, among other things, language, suicide, and waiting for Godot. Man's tragedy as seen here has, in fact, a double source—an internal one arising from his finite nature, and an external one in which that nature collides with the cosmos. Rightly or wrongly the average viewer perceives the play as one of horror without exaltation. His reaction to the scene that unfolds before him is one of horror and despair. He sympathizes, whether rightly or wrongly, with the characters, who may also have a feeling of horror and despair, although with them it must be considered largely subconscious. Be that as it may, by the close of the play he feels the despair and ennui of existence; he is made mindful of the foolishness of all activity between birth and death. In the foreline is a tendency toward death in the form of absolutes, withdrawal, a denial of life. The central irony of all this is that while the compromises depicted result in absurdity through their imprisoning consequences, correctives such as withdrawal result in absurdity through their freedom. And this freedom must be viewed as paradoxical freedom because it represents life apart from life, a kind of death-in-life. It is a kind of freedom that is isolationist, nihilistic, and irresponsible.[13]

Normally, we expect the tragic hero to suffer as a result of the predicament in which he has placed himself or in which the cosmos has placed him.[14] As we examine the reactions of the characters in *En attendant Godot* we find that they do indeed suffer, but the length, the degree, and the source of their suffering lead us to wonder whether it is of tragic proportions. Just as we have superficial physical comedy, so also do we have physical suffering, the most elementary kind of suffering. Estragon's feet hurt, he is hungry, he is beaten during the night. The messenger boy's brother, the sheepherder, is beaten. Vladimir, with his prostate condition, cannot laugh but only smile (thus physical suffering may hamper the comic response) and he has to urinate frequently (a source of amusement to Estragon). On the other hand, while we are horrified by the physical abuse heaped upon Lucky, we cannot help noticing that he himself does not in any way show signs of resentment. Yet he experiences anguish on another level when Pozzo threatens to get rid of him. However, from Pozzo's point of view, whatever sorrow Lucky feels over this is shortlived. This can be seen in the advice he gives to Estragon when the latter wishes to console Lucky, for he tells him to hurry up and do it, because he will soon stop crying

(p. 37). Indeed, so far as Pozzo is concerned, all states of suffering are momentary, and life is perpetually tossed between the tragic and the comic. He says, "Les larmes du monde sont immuables. Pour chacun qui se met à pleurer, quelque part un autre s'arrête. Il en va de même du rire"[15] (p. 38). ["The tears of the world are a constant quantity. For each one who begins to weep somewhere else another stops. The same is true of the laugh." (p. 22)] This contention of Pozzo seems to be borne out in the play by the fact that whatever spiritual anguish the characters experience appears to be of a fleeting nature. Pozzo's momentary anguish, which is generally oriented around the problem of pinpointing time, can be seen in the specific stage direction ("in an anguished voice") preceding his question as to whether it is evening (p. 98). The anguish of Estragon and Vladimir is equally fleeting. We see it in Estragon when he says such things as "I'm unhappy" and "I'm tired" which reflect his boredom and impatience. Vladimir's anguish is seen at moments when a lull in the divertissements occurs (p. 73, p. 96). Occasionally, too, Vladimir's ejaculations indicate mental suffering, as his "Miséricorde"(p. 107), which does not necessarily have to be construed as a response to the messenger's assertion that Godot's beard is white, but simply as a world-weary sigh of sorts.[16] Vladimir's anguish over Pozzo's treatment of Lucky is also quite temporary and his sympathies are easily diverted. Indeed the moods of all these men fluctuate, especially those of Vladimir and Estragon, so that at times Estragon's comic mask is momentarily replaced by the tragic mask, while the habitually tragic mask of Vladimir is sometimes supplanted by the comic.

However, is the suffering of these men commensurate with the gravity of the universal "mess," as Beckett calls it?[17] Do they think or speak of it? Do they feel anguish over it? Are they distressed by the notion that "We cannot know and we cannot be known"?[18] We believe that when all is said and done they do not experience profound suffering, and that they are just as ridiculous, and perhaps just as evil, as they are tragic. They are creatures who are willfully avoiding the basic issues of despair and death, and it is not unreasonable to think that Beckett views them as nontragic because they do not suffer to any significant degree. It is appropriate in this connection to recall what Beckett wrote about Proust's characters: "But already will, the will to live, the will not to suffer, Habit, having recovered from its momentary paralysis, has laid the foundations of its evil and necessary structure. . . ."[19] The quotation seems eminently applicable to Vladimir and Estragon, as well as to Pozzo and Lucky. Thus, we may safely say that as we do not have profound pain in the characters of *En attendant Godot,* so we cannot have the other pole, that of exaltation, that of tragic sublimity.[20]

Indeed, upon close scrutiny we discover that the nihilism, the ironies, the ambiguities portrayed in the play are probably not tragic in the eyes of Beckett, but are, rather, comic in a very special way. One might imagine Beckett is here indulging in what is described in *Watt* as the *risus purus,* or dianoetic laughter: " . . . the laugh of laughs. . . . the laugh laughing at the laugh, the beholding, the saluting of the highest joke, in a word, the laugh that laughs— silence please—at that which is unhappy."[21] This laughter, which is sardonic and mirthless, compounds the horror of the play by laughing at what is essentially evil—at the metaphysical condition of man as demonstrated through his many limitations.[22] Such laughter is basically nonsocial in nature. In conventional comedy the main character is ridiculed, usually for the purpose of bringing the erring "hero" back into society.[23] In *En attendant Godot,* however, Beckett is not ridiculing but mocking the main character, who is, in reality, a composite of all four characters—which is to say, the vast share of humanity.

Now, it is the rare person who ever reaches Beckett's level, that of the *risus purus.* Most of us are too involved with what we view as the tragic elements to have this particular perspective. Perhaps we also have habits in our concepts of tragedy and comedy that keep us from the greater suffering that comes from seeing humor in what is unhappy. We are tempted to sympathize with the characters, or else with their situation, when we should, perhaps, be holding them or it in disdain. This is partly why we, the audience, are viewed as being dead. Yet it is also highly improbable that Vladimir and Estragon have reached the level of *risus purus.* How, then, are they able to describe us as being dead? Are they the unconscious mouthpiece of Beckett in this matter? For it is quite clear that Beckett recognizes the situation (the absurdity of the human condition) as a source of the *risus purus,* or as he also calls it in *Watt,* the be-

holding of the "highest joke." He calls upon us to laugh at the attempt to gather meaning and purpose from that which has no meaning or purpose. This is black comedy at its blackest, in that it takes
a bitter view of the human being and of his condition. But does
Beckett include himself in this mockery of humanity? With such a
sardonic and pessimistic concept of man and having as he does the
idea that suffering is the main condition of the artistic experience,[24]
why does Beckett write?

There appear to be several answers to the question "Why does
Beckett write?"[25] First of all, he may write simply to divert others.
Then, too, he may write because he, like Didi and Gogo, must pass
the time. On the other hand, he may write to expose the chaotic
nature of man's situation, or else he may write so that one day he
may not have to write. Finally, he may write because being an artist
is a facet of his personality to which he must give expression. Or
the answer to this question may lie in a combination of these
reasons.

The first of these arguments—that he writes to divert others[26]—
can be illustrated by an example drawn from *En attendant Godot*
itself where we find Estragon and Vladimir being entertained by
Pozzo and Lucky. Vladimir and Estragon view this play-within-a-
play as pure divertissement. However, to interpret *Godot* solely in
this light would probably be a serious oversimplification because,
like Vladimir and Estragon, we would then be evading the basic
issues of death, ennui, finitude, disorder, etc., which are clearly
present in the play. In other words, to view Beckett's work as a
simple diversion could be to fall into the same pitfall as Vladimir
and Estragon. It would also be to take *En attendant Godot* as a
superficial comedy or as a pure tragedy, rather than as the complex
fusion of tragedy and comedy which it is.

Then again, we might compare Beckett to Malone, and say that
he writes to pass the time or to divert himself, a need which we
have seen to be dominant in Vladimir and Estragon, and a need
which all men have. This would be tantamount to talking aloud or
attempting to have a dialogue with society. But paradoxically, this
is in essence a monologue that you do for yourself and which others
inevitably distort. As Beckett himself writes, "Either we speak and
act for ourselves—in which case speech and action are distorted and

emptied of their meaning by an intelligence that is not ours, or else we speak and act for others—in which case we speak and act a lie."[27] Thus, this act of writing to pass time, which is a means of contending with solitude, results paradoxically in an even greater solitude, the solitude of the solipsist, brought about through the recognition that language inescapably separates a person from himself as well as from others.

On the other hand, and this is far more likely, Beckett may write to take inventory, as does Malone. Not only might he have as his goal to arrive at self-perception, but, more importantly, to expose the "mess"—the confusion everywhere present in man's existence. As he himself has stated in an interview with Tom Driver, "The only chance of renovation is to open our eyes and see the mess."[28] We have seen the portrayal of this chaos in the theology and morality of the characters in *En attendant Godot*. We have also seen it in the characters' physical and mental make-up as in their language. It is present in their relationships to one another as it also is in their use of time. The mixed tones of tragedy and comedy present in the play also contribute to the impression of confusion which we receive from the play.

This desire on the part of Beckett to expose the universal mess may be intended as a corrective ("a chance of renovation"), or it may be restricted to a mere mimesis, that is, to a presentation of the meaninglessness of life, in which case the play itself would have to be meaningless. But here a new irony would arise; for, as João Mendes has correctly asserted, the play is not meaningless, which would be proof that art and intelligence are not—as the play seeks to demonstrate—absurd.[29] That is to say, the need to express meaninglessness through meaningful form, and thus to give meaning, even though that meaning is meaninglessness, would constitute the greatest irony of all.

Then again, Beckett may be compelled to write in order to effect an exorcism;[30] that is, he may, like the character in *The Unnamable*, continue to talk so that one day he may be able to arrive at absolute silence.[31] What this would amount to is the desire of the literary artist to create the "perfect" work of art, a desire to make a full artistic and intellectual statement, but a desire which can, of course, never be fulfilled. This ideal work of art is Beckett's Godot, which he hopes for but can never attain, for he must necessarily distort his vision, whether he attempts to formulate it through language, with all its limitations, or through the mime, which, though less confining in one sense, is more so in another. The irony here is that Beckett knows that he cannot get at the perfect, undistorted art work, and yet he continues to try because he must.[32] Is his compulsion partially grounded in habit like the compulsions of Vladimir and Estragon?

Finally, Beckett may write because he is a series of individuals— a man, a thinker, a creative artist, etc.[33] As a thinker he has insights into the human condition, and, however pessimistic his views may be, for him art is the means by which he articulates these insights. Furthermore, as an artist, he is concerned with the solution of artistic problems which arise as he attempts to convey his world view. Thus the two facets of his personality—artist and thinker—interrelate and overlap one another.

Now, it is interesting to find Ashmore contending that art is the only thing not negated because not dealt with in *En attendant Godot*.[34] It is our belief, on the contrary, that aesthetic deliberations are manifold, perhaps paramount, in *En attendant Godot*, and that art is indeed negated. This can be observed in the dialogue of the characters as well as in the play's lack of conventional structure.

Although in *Proust* Beckett writes that "suffering opens a window on the real and is the main condition of the artistic experience,"[35] in *Godot* we find Estragon unable to transcend his life which is in a rut, his "roulure de vie au milieu des sables" (p. 70), unable to appreciate anything external to himself, such as a landscape ("fous-moi la paix avec tes paysages" [p. 71]), unwilling to grasp nuances (p. 70)—all of which things would be necessary for the appreciation or creation of art. His boredom—"Boredom that must be considered as the most tolerable because the most durable of human evils"[36]— obviates the possibility of an aesthetic experience.

On the other hand, certain abortive aesthetic responses on the part of Vladimir and Estragon can be found in the play. We might note for example their stilted, perhaps purely polite or mechanical, response to Pozzo's inquiry as to how they have found his speech on the night (p. 44). We might also note their angry reaction to the chaos and even to the content of Lucky's thinkpiece. Furthermore,

their ultimate response to the play-within-a-play—the beginning
and end of which are marked by the arrival and departure of Pozzo
and Lucky—is minimal in that they view it merely as a diversion,
as something which has helped to pass the time. In no way are they
moved to reflect on the horror of what they have just viewed; and,
if art ought to lead to a "renovation,"[37] then art is truly negated
here by Vladimir and Estragon. It is imperative to note that there
is a total degeneracy of art in Act II, for the play-within-a-play here
does not even result in the divertissement anticipated by Vladimir
upon the return of Pozzo and Lucky to the scene (p. 88).[38]

As we have seen before, the audience too is brought into the
realm of the play and thus we have in effect a play-within-a-play-
within-a-play. But in Act I the audience is viewed as a bog; hence,
like Estragon who says he is sunk in the mire and sand,[39] it is unable
to grasp the full intellectual and aesthetic portent of the play. Furthermore, in Act II the audience is viewed as being dead, hence
beyond hope of being reached by the artist.

The degeneracy of the theater suggested in the foregoing may be
attributed to the lethargy of the audience—to be compared to the
stagnation of Vladimir and Estragon—or to the difficulty the artist
has in presenting his ideas with any degree of immediacy, thus suggesting that art, especially art that has language as its medium, is
as limited as any other facet of man's existence.

This degeneracy of the theater is reflected in the antiformal nature of *En attendant Godot*. Let us not forget that the play has no
plot, thus no climax and no *dénouement;* it has no character development (no hero); and its genre is not clearcut. In other words, we
have a deformation of classical tragedy, a deformation of a conventional concept of the hero and a deformation of the stylistic devices
of the traditional drama. Thus, for example, if the vaudeville routines are to be likened to the Greek chorus, then these routines can
only be called a wretched parody of the choric interludes found in
the great classical plays. In addition, the events and the dialogue
presented are confused and chaotic, and intentionally so, for they
are meant to simulate the "mess" existing in reality. The use of the
antiplay, along with the withdrawal and rigidity or unchangingness
of the characters, is aesthetic nihilism, corresponding to Beckett's
nihilism and absolute nothingness as an ideal. There is a perfect

blending of *forme* and *fond* here: traditional form would have
blurred the nihilistic world view present in the play. Yet, once again
we find irony in the fact that the play, though it may intend to ne-
gate theater (art), nevertheless is a play, nevertheless does have
form, just as the motifs built on the meaninglessness and futility of
life are charged with meaning. Thus, almost in spite of the artist,
decomposition is replaced by innovation and renovation, old form
is replaced by new form, and, in a sense, an old vision of man is
replaced by a new one.

It is highly doubtful that *En attendant Godot* has a moral message
in any obvious sense. Beckett, like the contemporary dramatist described by Stratford, assumes all the roles: judge, accused, and
witnesses.[40] This is the kind of irony—the pathos of the middle—
discussed by Hopper, and, as Hopper points out, the ironist escapes
the need to moralize.[41] Instead, Beckett merely presents the human situation as he sees it. As a result of this, neither tragic nor
comic catharsis is present in the play. It may be that Beckett condemns the human condition, but it cannot be said that he gives us
either a remedy or a corrective. The play is in no way didactic; it
does not intend to "correct" or to chastise. Beckett, in his intention
to expose the chaos and finitude of man's existence through this
play, is supporting his view expressed in his conversation with Tom
F. Driver, in which Beckett is reported to have said, "The only
chance of renovation is to open our eyes and see the mess. It is not
a mess you can make sense of."[42] As at almost every turn in the
road, here again we come upon an irony; for it is not difficult to see
that, in presenting a pessimistic and nihilistic view of man through
this antiplay, there is an implicit moral stand.

It remains to be known whether man is able to escape the suffering, however great or however little, which arises from this
"mess" as it is described by Beckett, not only in his interview with
Driver but also in his writings. It would appear that it can be done
through art—Vladimir and Estragon are able to do this temporarily.
It would also appear that it can be done through laughter. And this
leads us to another point.

We have pointed out three stages in the establishment of the
genre of the play: the superficially comic, the tragic, and the sardonic. These stages might also represent levels of aesthetic aware-

ness in both the audience and Beckett. At the level of superficial laughter we have a response of pure pleasure devoid of pain. At the next level pain enters into the response, pain mixed with horror and despair. This is the response that could lead to greater understanding than the first could give, if we were able to objectify sufficiently. Thus this response must be absorbed into the third level, where we are able to stand off from the tragic situation and laugh at it. In other words, it would seem that Beckett wishes us to get the distance he apparently has from the content of the play; he appears to want to shake us out of our complacency, out of our sentimentality; he evidently wants to make us uncomfortable.

The efforts made in this chapter to answer the question as to why Beckett writes may not be satisfactory, but the question is there to be answered, and we have attempted to cope with it by providing possible answers drawn from Beckett's own work. Whatever the answer may be, the question is an important one whenever the deprecation of art and indeed of human dignity is involved. To avoid the question would be to dismiss Beckett as nothing but a "successful peddler of despair."[43]

Despite the fact that one might come away from *En attendant Godot* with the idea that the theater is dead, the fact remains that the theater may well be able to perform a function which philosophy no longer seems to be performing. That is to say, the theater might enable us to better understand our condition and might even provide us with the *aide-à-vivre* which philosophy once gave us but no longer appears to do. How literature (and particularly *En attendant Godot*) might accomplish the goals of philosophy or might fail to do this will be the subject of our final chapter.

PHILOSOPHY AND LITERATURE

Gustav E. Mueller's statement that "There is more significant philosophy in the American novel than there is in the output of our philosophy departments"[1] might well be extended to include twentieth-century European and American literature in general. We have in the preceding six chapters seen how *En attendant Godot* has philosophical content which may indeed be of as much or more significance than the philosophy being done by "our philosophy departments." However, the task remains before us to relate Beckett to philosophers, especially contemporary philosophers, but only with the purpose of showing how the play retains its identity as a work of art and how it is different from a philosophical treatise. Allied to this task is the equally important one of presenting a critique of Beckett's world view and of showing the relationship between this world view and the aesthetic values of the play, or, in other words, the connection between the content and the form. In this chapter we propose not only to accomplish these tasks, but to draw our study to a close by commenting upon the procedures we have adopted in our analysis of *En attendant Godot,* and upon the aesthetic problems which they raise. Here we will detect a central irony which will only serve to illustrate how right Beckett's view of man may turn out to be.

Though Mueller's remark may be somewhat exaggerated, it does point up certain trends in contemporary philosophy and literature. In the first place, the statement is aimed at contemporary analytic philosophy, which, being technical, is philosophy for philosophers.

That is, analytic philosophy, which is confined to the examination of the meaning of concepts,[2] does not concern itself with "questions of 'belief,'—questions of a religious, moral, political, or generally 'cosmic' variety."[3] Hence, analytic philosophy provides neither an *aide-à-vivre* nor a *Weltanschauung*. In addition it does not help us, except in a remote sense, to understand our existence, at least not in the manner in which Aristotle claims that tragedy can do,[4] and in which *En attendant Godot* appears to do. Perhaps, then, some contemporary art, though it may not offer an *aide-à-vivre*, does help us to understand our existential plight, because the connections between this art and life per se are more readily apparent than are those between analytic philosophy and human experience.

Mueller's position is, furthermore, strengthened by the fact that many contemporary existentialist philosophers have deemed it necessary to turn to metaphorical devices, often expressed through established literary genres, to give a fuller or more adequate expression of their philosophical views. Moreover, the reverse of this picture is the case with Beckett, who, though he has never written a philosophical tract, nevertheless presents us with a rather complete *Weltanschauung*, which permeates not only *En attendant Godot* but all his other works as well. Moreover, this *Weltanschauung*, though it has certain themes in common with former as well as contemporary philosophers, arrives at different conclusions from theirs.

In other words, Beckett's pessimistic and nihilistic world view is the outgrowth of concern for problems which are not peculiar to him, but have plagued writers and philosophers of the past as well as other contemporaries of his. He shares with Malraux, Sartre, Camus, and Ionesco a sense of the absurdity of human existence, even though the manner in which the problem is articulated is at variance and even though some of these writers offer a resolution which is lacking in Beckett. In addition, Beckett, like his contemporaries (Gide, Camus, Sartre, etc.) doubts existing moral values; but with Beckett there is no suggestion of revolt, because, due to his skepticism, revolt would be of no more value than stagnation, for revolt would not change man. Beckett does not seek to substitute one set of values for another. Instead, he is intent upon showing the conflict of moral values. That is to say, the chaos in the moral realm (as everywhere else) makes it impossible for us to know with any certainty good from evil, right from wrong, and so forth. Man with his finitude and limitations cannot evolve a systematic morality, and even if he were able to do so, one system would not be preferable to another. Moral systems are evolved for the good life, to make life worth living, to give life meaning, and in Beckett's opinion man will never be able to overcome the meaninglessness of life, nor the absurdity of death which contributes in large part to this meaninglessness.

Hence, Beckett's primary concern is not an ethical-aesthetic one, but rather a metaphysical-aesthetic one: he is concerned with a portrayal of the "mess," and from this portrayal we infer man's metaphysical limitations, ethical, epistemological, etc. This stress on the metaphysical is profoundly philosophical, in spite of the fact that Ross appears to hold conversely that what renders a piece of literature philosophical is its stress on the *ethical* and not the metaphysical.[5]

Now, Beckett's view of the metaphysical condition of man, which we have seen to be a very gloomy one—relieved only by great craftsmanship[6]—is inevitably distorted because of its concentration on the negative; and yet distortion, be it negative or positive, is something which is manifested not only in any writer, but also in any metaphysician. As Bergson has assured us, the domain of existence is richer than any of our limited schemes.[7] Hence, Beckett is as limited as any of the characters he conceives, in all their limitations. This is only one more of the many ironies we have been noting in the course of this study.

Thus, it is quite possible to turn Beckett's view of man as it is implied in *En attendant Godot* onto Beckett himself, by demonstrating that the view he presents is applicable to him, a finite and limited man, whose philosophy has all the distortions present in any thinker or writer. His normal procedure is to see the negative and to omit the positive. For example, he views habit as a great *"sourdine,"* which it can be; but, on the other hand, habit or routine not only preserves and unifies life, but can even be construed as that which gives meaning to life. In other words, from a dialectical point of view, work—to take a concrete example of something grounded in habit or routine—may be regarded not only as the means of pro-

viding the necessities of life, but as that which gives order and purpose to life, as Beckett's writing possibly and even probably does
for him. Similarly, memory, which Beckett apparently views as extremely faulty, is an ordering factor without which we would not
have habit (with all its negative and positive values) or reasoning
powers. And in spite of the defectiveness Beckett seems to associate
with reason, it is by reason that we may see reason's limitations.
Besides, reason is the tool which enables man to prolong his life;
it has allowed man to achieve the technology necessary to get him
to the moon—assuming that these accomplishments are ideals and
that the problems that such accomplishments create can ultimately
be overcome. Furthermore, language, which Beckett views as de-
ficient, is one of the principal vehicles for expressing rational and
artistic activity, and, despite everything, communication does come
about through it. Thus, ironically enough, it is through language
itself that Beckett exhibits for us the limitations of language and it
is through reason that he shows the limitations of reason, though
we would have to admit that through an additional irony Beckett
is only too well aware of this fact. And though Beckett regards the
body as limited and finite, presenting it in its most degraded and
debilitated condition, as a thing which is declining in size and power
(see Lucky's speech), there are those who would argue that it is a
very nearly miraculous organism and a medium capable of great
athletic and aesthetic feats. Finally, the nihilism and pessimism of
Beckett, which admit in the realm of social intercourse only solitude
or in its place only cruel or ambivalent fraternity,[8] are to be con-
trasted with the concepts of fruitful fraternity and unanimity we find
in a Camus or a Teilhard de Chardin.[9] Now, though the refutation
of these counterarguments could dialectically lead us back to
Beckett's viewpoint, nevertheless the positive side of each of these
issues exists, and it is difficult to find Beckett recognizing this anywhere in his writings.

Yet this concentration on the negative is not peculiar to Beckett.
He shares his skepticism with as ancient a philosopher as the Soph-
ist Gorgias who held that nothing exists and that even if something
did exist it could not be known, and even if it could be known it
could not be communicated. As we have shown, Beckett maintains
much the same position in *En attendant Godot*, where existence is

viewed as illusory, and where the ability to know or to communicate what might be known are both pictured as highly doubtful. But Beckett's skepticism is even more sophisticated than that of Gorgias, reflecting as it does developments in philosophy later than Gorgias. Among these are his adoption of the Cartesian mind/body dualism, and his skepticism regarding various philosophers' endeavors to demonstrate a union of the two.[10] Yet the gloominess inherent in this thorough-going skepticism is transcended by a rejection of the attitude of the "lachrymose philosopher" Heraclitus in favor of that of the laughing philosopher Democritus. This is, of course, related to the fusion of tragedy and comedy; and the fact that Beckett adopts the attitude of Democritus is merely another way of saying that he adopts the *risus purus* in the face of the universal mess.[11]

Beckett not only reflects the thinking of ancient philosophers, but, as we have already hinted, he writes squarely in the twentieth century, concerning himself with many of the same subjects as most of the contemporary existentialist philosophers. Chief among these subjects is the role of death (and suicide) in human existence. The two philosophers with whom it is most profitable to compare Beckett in this respect are Heidegger and Camus; for in Sartre it is not death but freedom which is the source of anguish and authentic being.

Throughout this study we have been noting that the characters of *En attendant Godot* assiduously avoid any real confrontation with death. Now, it is this very confrontation with the void which is the one unique experience of the human being, thus the unique source of authentic being for Heidegger. Inasmuch as our characters remain largely in the domain of forfeiture, that is, are tied to the distractions of everyday habit (the present) they cannot resolve to have a destiny. And it is the resolution to face death, to absorb birth and to make one's destiny which in Heidegger's philosophy allows one to transcend the realm of forfeiture and to rise to one's proper stature, that is, the realm of authentic being. Now, to cling to the world of things—the domain of forfeiture—and to refuse to probe into the question of being is to Heidegger the very essence of nihilism. Hence we may safely say that in *En attendant Godot* we are presented with a fundamentally nihilistic approach to existence, and

although Heidegger himself offers us the somewhat unusual defi-
nition of nihilism given just above, his theory that we must face the
nothingness of death in order to arrive at authentic being and his
mystical concepts of silence as the ultimate replacement of speech
can also be construed as nihilistic. In this case, it might be con-
tended that Beckett's nihilism is even more pessimistic than that
of Heidegger, since there is some question for Beckett as to whether
man, with all his limitations, has the means of attaining authentic
being. That Beckett appears to think that there is, if not authentic
being, at least an essential self can be granted; but for him one can
neither arrive at nor get rid of this self.

Now, if we turn to Camus as a point of comparison with Beckett,
we again find striking similarities and yet significant differences.
Chief among these similarities is a preoccupation with suicide. As
is well known, for Camus suicide is the only truly serious philosophical question which man must ask himself. It is not death, then,
that is the crux of Camus' position, but life. That is, one must decide
whether life has intrinsic value despite its apparent meaninglessness
or its apparent lack of future. Camus arrives at the conclusion that
it is not legitimate to take one's life because this would be to deny
the one irreplaceable possession one has. Thus, by an assertion of
the intrinsic value of life, the absurdity of death is transcended, and
man has found the means to proceed beyond the limits of nihilism,
as Camus contends can be done.[12] Beckett, on the other hand,
shows through *En attendant Godot* a somewhat different idea of
suicide. By now, it is obvious that the characters in our play entertain the idea of suicide, but never seriously consider it as an alternative to their condition of ennui. This is because they lack the
means and the conviction. For them the notion of taking their lives
is merely one more game among many. Their suicide would not be
an affirmation of the value of life, any more than it is for Beckett
himself. Creatures of habit that they are, Vladimir and Estragon do
have glimmers of the ennui resulting from this habit, but this very
habit has dulled them to the point that they cannot assert the absurdity of habit by committing suicide. In other words, they postpone their suicide not because they have recognized that life is their
dearest gift, not because they have recognized the absurdity of their
meaningless existence, but they "continue making the gestures

commanded by existence for many reasons, the first of which is habit."[13] There is no indication here or in any of Beckett's other works that death must be avoided because life itself is worth living. Indeed there is no apparent reason for "continuing" (the hypothetical imperative found in most of Beckett's works), but yet there is a constant thrust toward an achievement of certain absolutes which would constitute a death-in-life, one step away from literal, physical death. The problem is circular, however, because the nihilist's dreams for such absolutes as total silence, total immobility, the perfect work of art, etc., cannot be attained. One must conclude that although both Camus and Beckett have strains of stoicism and a preoccupation with suicide in common, the world view of Beckett differs even more from that of Camus than it does from that of Heidegger. This is because Beckett is fundamentally nihilistic and pessimistic, neither of which can be properly ascribed to Camus with his conviction that life is worth living and that when all is said and done, "The struggle itself toward the heights is enough to fill a man's heart. One must imagine Sisyphus happy."[14]

The links that we find between Beckett and these philosophers make us wonder what the procedures of Beckett, a literary artist whose work has philosophical implications, have or do not have in common with the procedures of a metaphysician.

When we examine this question closely, we find that Beckett, like a metaphysician, seeks to present us with a synthesis or a total vision of man. But, to repeat, he fails in this enterprise just as the metaphysician does, because in both cases the vision is a result of selection and over-emphasis, and so both give us a distorted view of man. For example, in their articulation of an exaggerated skepticism both Beckett and Gorgias assume what they deny. That is to say, both of them take for granted the power of language to communicate their disbelief in the efficacy of language.[15] Both of them also take for granted that they have arrived at a certain amount of knowledge about the universe, which knowledge they hold to be an impossibility, but which knowledge they nevertheless intend to communicate through their special vision of the universe.

One of the results of this distortion is that in their effort to overcome it, philosophers and artists devise alternate and very frequently incompatible world views. And Walsh's statement that it is possible through a "willing suspension of disbelief" to accept two incompatible truths in art, while in philosophy a choice must be made,[16] does not seem entirely satisfactory. For while we can *appreciate* incompatible truths in either art or philosophy, we cannot *believe in* incompatible world views whether presented by an artist or by a philosopher. In other words, we can appreciate the philosophies of both Hegel and Hobbes, where it is not possible to believe in both simultaneously, just as it is possible to appreciate such differing plays as Beckett's *En attendant Godot* and Claudel's *L'Annonce faite à Marie*, while it is quite impossible to espouse at the same time the pessimistic world view of the one, which sets in doubt the possibility of salvation, and the ultimately optimistic world view of the other, which has at its source an orthodox Christian concept of salvation.

An explanation for the above phenomenon may be that while we do not adopt the ideas of the art work we can admire its craftsmanship, as we can admire the philosophic work for its skillful argumentation. In either case the form is an organic part of the vision.[17] During this study it has become clear that the technical features of *En attendant Godot* cannot be separated from Beckett's vision of the universal mess in which man is embedded. Similarly, the evolution of Plato's philosophy is reflected in the modifications he makes in the dialogue form so that it may conform with the development of his philosophic ideas. And while we expect consistency and coherence between form and content in both the literary artist and the philosopher, this consistency does not always come about in the manner described by Amy Kleppner when she writes:

> That the discursive philosophical writing and works of imaginative literature share some properties seems apparent. We demand of both, for example, a degree of consistency or coherence. We do not expect the philosopher to assert proposition 'p' on one page and to deny the same proposition on the next. Similarly we assume that ideally the literary artist will not present incredible changes of character, will not at some point repudiate descriptive statements made earlier, will not allow the names of persons and places to shift in the course of a given work.[18]

Now, while what Kleppner says about consistency and coherence in philosophical writing is true, it is valuable to point out once again that the coherence and consistency of *En attendant Godot* rest if anywhere in the abundant use of inconsistency and incoherence to portray the chaos of life. And it is to be noted that in the process of disclosing this chaos Beckett does indeed "allow the names and places to shift." Furthermore, the repetitiveness, over-elaboration, and verbosity which appear to Kleppner to be anathema in a literary or philosophic work can be devices which are intentional and quite appropriate to the expression of certain world views. Certainly here again we have observed repetitiveness, for instance, used by Beckett not only for comic effects, but, more profoundly, for the purpose of exhibiting the tedium and ennui of human existence. The same principles apply for any verbosity and over-elaboration which may be discerned in the play.

Thus, Kleppner's effort to point out similarities between the writer and the metaphysician is not entirely satisfactory. Perhaps, on the other hand, a glance at the differences might shed more light on the matter, and indeed it is these differences which largely concern us here.

For, even though Beckett has much in common with the philosophic approach, *En attendant Godot* is a play and not a piece of philosophical writing. By this we mean that the metaphysical vision is encapsulated in the artistic vision. Whatever Beckett's aim is, it is certainly not to make claims and to justify them with tightly constructed arguments. Instead, he is presenting the human condition as he sees it in a concrete situation; he displays and exhibits, where the philosopher asserts.[19] Thus, while the philosopher presents us with ready-made theories and generalizations, in the case of *Godot* we must infer the generalizations. This is not to say that literature does not have cognitive content.[20] Neither is it to say that the philosopher does not give us examples, or does not use metaphor or analogy; but examples and metaphors are used by the philosopher to clarify, not to imitate. Beckett, on the other hand, imitates (though he does not directly copy) the "universal mess." He himself recognizes the need to find the appropriate example for illustrating this "mess" when he says in the Driver interview, "To find a form that accommodates the mess, that is the task of the artist now."[21] By extension, the example with which we are dealing displays the human condition in such a way that our emotions are liable to become involved, while were this a philosophical treatise we would find the condition discussed in nonemotive language or in discursive language which sought to present an argumentation or justification of its point of view.

In short, *En attendant Godot* has something in common with what Amy Kleppner finds to be true of the literary works of Sartre and Camus, where, according to her, we get a particular conception of the human condition articulated in a manner which is perhaps even more adequate than would have been the case had it been expressed in discursive philosophy.[22] Consequently, sometimes literature may supply if not an *aide-à-vivre* at least an expressive incarnation of certain insights into life in a manner not possible in philosophical discourse. The result of this phenomenon may be that the human situation can be portrayed with such poignancy and such magnitude that the reader or spectator will react more strongly than he would when confronted with philosophical texts. As a result, he will be more inclined to act, to change, to be more or less tolerant as the case may be, and so forth. In other words, whether the author intends it or not, a piece of literature can have the effect of catharsis, while this is an unlikely effect when it comes to a philosophical piece.

We have noted in previous sections of this chapter that the form and the content of *En attendant Godot*, as of all literary works, are inseparable.[23] Now, if this is the case, how can we justify the type of analysis we have made, which has entailed just such a separation? The answer to this question is at once simple and complex. It is impossible to talk about the totality of a literary work, and so, in order to analyze it, we are forced to separate its constituent parts. And if we are to reveal the philosophical profundity of a play such as *Godot* we are forced into analysis. We are also forced into analysis if we are to acquire any degree of understanding of any work, and especially of a play as difficult as is *En attendant Godot*. While some might argue that analysis not only will not bring about an understanding of a work, but might even diminish one's aesthetic enjoyment of it, it is our belief that an awareness of the manner in which the work is constructed—both from the ideological and the technical points of view—will bring about a richer appreciation of it. Furthermore, just as the author seeks to articulate his world view as he understands it (and perhaps seeks to understand the world

through the act of articulation) so the reader (or spectator), in analyzing and reflecting on the piece of literature, not only comes to
understand it better, but perhaps also comes to understand himself
and his world better.[24]

The question that now arises is how shall the reader come to the
"proper" understanding of the work. For, assuming that the work
is not ambiguous, and perhaps even if it is ambiguous, "proper"
understanding involves the correct inference of beliefs, ideas, tone,
etc. from the clues presented by the author. The obvious danger
is that what is inferred may not be what is implied.

A related danger is that even if the reader correctly identifies
what is implied, the philosophical implications of the work may not
be "true"; they may be exaggerated or distorted, and under these
circumstances the reader must put the world view of the artist into
proper perspective. It has been our intention to do just this in presenting alternatives to Beckett's *Weltanschauung* toward the beginning of this chapter.

It would appear from the above discussion that we believe there
is one "ideal" interpretation of a work of art. And in a certain way
of looking at the problem, this is true. It appears to us that insofar
as there is only one world view informing the work of art, for two
critics to find within the one work two contradictory world views
suggests that one of the two critics has failed to take into account
all of the clues, but has instead selected a group of clues that enable
him to sustain his theory of the meaning of the work. This, of
course, does not preclude the possibility of multi-dimensional interpretations, provided that they are in harmony with one another.
Such a possibility as this arises not only from the ambiguities of the
art work itself, but also from the particular question a given critic
may ask himself.[25] In the long run, however, it seems that these
multi-dimensional interpretations must be directed toward a single
depth meaning (an ideal meaning), and that those interpretations
which do not disclose this have either held too closely to isolated
facets of the work, rather than attempting to deal with its totality,
or have been interrupted at a level or more short-of-the-depth
meaning.[26] Thus it is possible to interpret *En attendant Godot* as
a farce, but this would remain a superficial assessment of the play.
Similarly, it is possible to construe it as a tragedy but this, too,

would be to fail to see the profound cynicism and lack of faith in man which divert the potential tragedy of the play. Yet, even though we strongly believe that the probable depth meaning is the one we have set forth, as it takes into account as much as is possible the combined form and content of the play, we hasten to add that an "ideal" interpretation of this play, or of any literary work, is an absolute because it is unrealizable. Arriving at the "correct" interpretation does not depend, as Weitz is said to have claimed, upon the determination of the best critical method or category of explanation.[27] Rather it is beyond attainment.

Beckett, in his play *En attendant Godot*, has displayed not only the universal mess, but man's inability to cope with it, and with the fact of death, because of his finite nature and to the faultiness of his tools. Ironically Beckett the artist partakes of these limitations, and as a result his art may present a world view which is not only a distortion of his own world view and artistic vision, but even a distortion of "reality" itself. The supreme irony is that the critic like the artist is heir to this finitude. He, too, must work with inadequate tools (method, language, memory, etc.). Ultimately, he is unable to speak of the totality of the work; he must separate form and content, which inevitably distorts the work of art, as he, like the literary artist, must articulate his thoughts through language, and thus distort his own meanings. If the artist distorts, the critic is in the position of distorting a distortion. However, this is the only critical apparatus we have, and we must use it if we are to reveal (although distorting) Beckett's presentation of the universal mess.

It is conceivable, then, that we have arrived at the wrong depth meaning of *En attendant Godot*, and as a result—if one follows Weitz[28]—have drawn out of the play a set of universal principles which are in reality not in the play. This would be because at best the depth meaning of a literary work is ordinarily only implicit, as is the case with *Godot*. But the subject of universality is in itself one which poses many problems. Does the universal as such exist? If so, does it exist in art? And if it does, how do we identify it? Efforts to answer these and related questions would fill another book.

NOTES

Introduction

1. Lawrence E. Harvey, *Samuel Beckett, Poet and Critic* (Princeton: Princeton University Press, 1970), p. 421.

2. David Helsa's *The Shape of Chaos: An Interpretation of the Art of Samuel Beckett* (Minneapolis: The University of Minnesota Press, 1971) is a study devoted to a comparison of Beckett's ideas with those of ancient and contemporary philosphers and thinkers. This work appeared after our study was completed. We have since examined it and find that it complements in large measure our discussion of such problems as time and the identity of Godot. However, Helsa's identification of Godot as "Time Future," the "Possible Absolute," and as "the Answer to which the being of man is the Question" (pp. 134–35) leads him to conclusions that are incompatible with our view that Godot is not God. But despite this incompatibility, his version of Godot as a being who is only *possible* points to the futility of waiting for a never-to-be-actualized being, and thus reinforces our interpretation of Beckett's view of man, as depicted in *En attendant Godot*.

3. The French edition used throughout this study is that of Germaine Brée and Eric Schoenfeld: Samuel Beckett, *En attendant Godot* (New York: The Macmillan Company, 1963). All page and line references are to this edition, unless otherwise indicated. The English text will be given in the footnotes for the longer and more vital quotes. It will be taken from Samuel Beckett's *Waiting for Godot* (New York: Grove Press, 1954), and the page numbers following the English text will refer to this edition. The concept of atonement for birth is found in *Godot*, p. 12, "se repentir d'être né."

See also Beckett in *Proust* (New York: Grove Press, 1931), p. 49. Jacobsen and Mueller, among others, study this problem in their *Testament of Samuel Beckett* (New York: Hill & Wang, 1964), p. 105.

4. See G. S. Fraser in *Casebook on Waiting for Godot*, ed. Ruby Cohn (New York: Grove Press, 1967), pp. 133–37 for an interpretation of *En attendant Godot* as a Christian allegory, and especially p. 134 where he writes, "*Waiting for Godot* . . . is a modern morality play on permanent Christian themes." See also C. Chadwick, "Waiting for Godot: A Logical Approach," *Symposium*, vol. XIV, no. 4 (Winter, 1960), pp. 252–57.

Chapter 1

1. Gunther Anders, "Being Without Time," in *Samuel Beckett, a Collection of Critical Essays*, ed. Martin Esslin (Englewood Cliffs, N. J.: Prentice-Hall, Inc., 1965), p. 141.

2. From Colin Duckworth's article, "The Making of Godot" (in *Casebook*, op. cit., p. 89 ff.), we learn that in the manuscript version of the play Estragon is named Lévy. Hence the Vladimir-Estragon duo archaically represented the Judeo-Christian tradition with all the tensions implicit in this. Beckett's change here suggests his desire to remove the play from too strict a religious interpretation.

3. The mind/body problem as a theme is not restricted to *En attendant Godot*, but appears in many other works of Beckett, especially the trilogy.

4. This is a type of pairing off that often occurs in the works of Beckett. Compare, for example, *All That Fall, Endgame*, etc.

5. Estragon (speaking of the "new" shoes): "Elles sont trop grandes." Vladimir: "Tu auras peut-être des chaussettes un jour." (p. 80) In English: "They're too big. Perhaps you'll have socks some day." (p. 45)

6. He says as much (p. 13), and tells Pozzo that his name is Catulle (p. 43). This name not only suggests the Catullus of antiquity, but is perfectly conceivable in a modern context, as in the name of the Parnassian poet Catulle Mendès (1841–1909). When in the English version he claims to Pozzo that his name is Adam (p. 25), we are drawn away from the notion of his being a poet and are drawn toward the one of everyman as well as toward the theological notion of the Judeo-Christian heritage existing in the ur-text where he is called Lévy.

7. For further considerations on the mind/body problem in Beckett's works see Hugh Kenner's "The Cartesian Centaur" (in Esslin, op. cit., pp. 52–61). Also see Ruby Cohn's "Philosophical Fragments in the Works of Samuel Beckett," (in Esslin, pp. 169–177), and John Fletcher, *Samuel Beckett's Art* (London: Chatto and Windus, 1967), pp. 126–31.

8. And yet upon occasion Vladimir points out to Estragon faulty reasoning on his part. For example, see p. 48, lines 7–17.

9. See the reason for committing suicide as a "moyen de bander" (p. 19); also note the effects of Vladimir's prostate condition.

10. The authors recognize that falling and stumbling are comic devices, but see in these physical manifestations profound implications, nevertheless.

11. This, of course, is an ancient source of comedy. It is also a significant memory lapse, because Pozzo, unlike Vladimir and Estragon, is not waiting for Godot.

12. See Sue Ellen Case, for instance, in *Casebook* (op. cit.), p. 158. Also see Edith Kern, "Beckett and the Spirit of the *Commedia dell'arte,*" *Modern Drama*, vol. 9, no. 3 (December 1966), pp. 260–67. The dialogue between Vladimir and Estragon in which they liken the Pozzo-Lucky encounter to the "spectacle," the "music-hall," the "cirque," together with Vladimir's "Garde ma place" said to Estragon as he departs to urinate all suggest this notion that we have here a play-within-a-play (p. 40).

13. Compare Hamm (in *Endgame*) who dominates from his wheelchair placed squarely in the middle of the room.

14. "They" beat Estragon. Vladimir and Estragon have "gotten rid of their rights." See Jacques Guicharnaud, *Modern French Theatre from Giraudoux to Genêt* (New Haven: Yale University Press, 1968), p. 237.

15. The present discussion is not indebted to a treatment of the mind/body problem to be found in John Rechtien, "Time and Eternity Meet in the Present," *Texas Studies in Literature and Language,* vol. VI, no. 1 (Spring, 1964), p. 12 and p. 20, where the Lucky-Pozzo pair represent body/mind or the bad thief (belonging to the scientific myth) and Estragon-Vladimir represent body/mind or the good thief (belonging to the Christian myth). The argument that one of these pairs is to be saved and the other not does not appear to us to be tenable. Furthermore, it is our feeling that Rechtien refutes his own thesis on the final page of his article. The conversation between Vladimir and Estragon concerning the good thief and the bad is treated in the section of this study dealing with time.

16. The games become more frequent in Act II, perhaps reflecting the fact that the situation is more desperate; thus the activity grows more frantic.

17. It is interesting to note that the interaction of the relationship between Estragon and Vladimir once was clear to them, and now has grown hazy. ("Dos à dos, comme au bon vieux temps." p. 85.)

18. Pozzo appears to have more than one "man": "Il se figure que je vais regretter ma décision. Tel est son misérable calcul. Comme si j'étais à court d'hommes de peine" (p. 36). In English: "He imagines that when I see him

indefatigable I'll regret my decision. Such is his miserable scheme. As though I were short of slaves!" (p. 21) Or is this mere braggadocio on the part of the pompous Pozzo?

19. See Chadwick, op. cit., p. 253, where he maintains that Pozzo is Godot, a theory we cannot wholly endorse for reasons that will be seen later on in this study. He further suggests (pp. 256–57) that Pozzo's and Lucky's helplessness in Act II may be a great joke, a joke played by the Divinity on man, and that Pozzo and Lucky may be feigning blindness and dumbness. Chadwick bases this argument on Vladimir's "It seemed to me that he saw us." (See p. 105, lines 2–12 of the play.) But this could be a manifestation of Vladimir's skepticism. (See p. 58 of the play.) Estragon and Vladimir wonder just as tellingly about what day of the week it is, whether it is dawn or dusk, etc. All of Chadwick's quotations seem to us to have to do with doubt, with the human being's inability to know anything for sure. Similarly, Chadwick's argument that Pozzo appears to think Lucky can talk (p. 100, l. 16 of the play) may be attributed to the faulty memory he has already confessed to having (p. 45 of the play). Memory and skepticism will be discussed by us in Chapters Two and Three of the present study.

20. Guicharnaud, op. cit., p. 244.

21. In that Estragon and Vladimir are observers of Pozzo and Lucky, who can be said to be "acting out" life, the former are analogous to Beckett himself, who stands away from his characters as he does from life and watches the performance as if he were not a victim, whereas in point of fact he is.

22. The scene in which all four men are lying on the stage in a heap has been shown by Edith Kern to be a *commedia dell'arte lazzo*, as are the exchange of hats, and other routines. (Edith Kern, op. cit., p. 262) We are less concerned here with comic and theatrical effects (though such an interpretation is equally valid and not in contradiction). Our concern here is with the symbolic implications of the various gestures and speeches.

23. It is pertinent to point out that Lucky probably never wants to be alone, though ironically he more than any of the others might be better off if he were alone. Perhaps he is somehow aware that it is now too late for separation from Pozzo, that his dependency upon him is now so great and so habitual that he would not survive apart from Pozzo.

24. See in relation to this André Marissel, *Beckett* (Paris: Classiques du XXe siècle, Editions Universitaires, 1963), p. 60: "Le personnage beckettien, homosexuel plus ou moins déguisé, qui, de son propre aveu, sucerait encore les tétons de sa nourrice, en est resté en fait à l'onanisme."

25. In his discussion of the past, he maintains that in 1900—which was an eternity ago—"on portait beau . . . Maintenant il est trop tard" (pp. 10–

11). We know too that the pair is well past their prime by the remark of Estragon, later in the play, "Dos à dos comme au bon vieux temps!" (p. 85), and by the fact that Estragon and Vladimir have been together some fifty years (p. 63).

26. The slang meaning of the word *navet* (penis) should not be overlooked in this context either.

27. The father-son relationship to be seen in the friendship of Vladimir and Estragon finds its echo in the case of Pozzo and Lucky, but in the latter this relationship is too ambiguous to be called abnormal; for even though on the surface it appears that Pozzo is the tyrannical father type, Lucky is in a certain sense the historical father, from whom Pozzo has learned all the beautiful things, all the nuances of life (p. 38). It is only by chance that their stations in life are what they presently are, with the bald-headed Pozzo wielding the whip and Lucky, perhaps the younger with his full head of hair, responding to Pozzo's every order.

28. Though rationally inclined, Vladimir himself verbalizes a skepticism concerning human reason when, in discussing the need to fill time with acts, he says to Estragon: "Tu me diras que c'est pour empêcher notre raison de sombrer. C'est une affaire entendue. Mais n'erre-t-elle pas déjà dans la nuit permanente des grands fonds, voilà ce que je me demande parfois." He concludes this observation on the absurdity of our time-fillers which masquerade as reasonable acts with the ironical question, "Tu suis mon raisonnement?" (p. 92).

Chapter 2

1. See in the play Vladimir's statement that the one thing that is clear is that "we" (that is, all of us) are waiting for Godot. "Nous attendons. Nous nous ennuyons" (pp. 91–92).

2. The fact that this statement is in Latin may tell us something about Vladimir's past (his education), as well as something about his memory. Moreover, the presence of this Latin quotation evokes the pedant of the French farce and of the *commedia dell'arte* tradition.

3. The mild scatology contained in this particular speech manifestation is, of course, another source of comedy. The language of *En attendant Godot* will be discussed in detail in Chapter Four.

4. At the beginning of Lucky's speech he speaks of an aphasiac god. This god whom Lucky is describing has some of Lucky's characteristics, which characteristics leave the "personal god" of whom Lucky speaks paradoxically anthropomorphic and yet unable to communicate with man.

5. The use of the term 'voluntary memory' in the present study is based on Beckett's use of the term in *Proust* (New York: Grove Press, 1931). The whole subject of memory as treated in this chapter and the one following obviously invites comparison with Proust, among others; but such a comparison, however tempting it might be, would unfortunately carry us rather far from the scope of the study at hand, specifically Beckett's concept of the memory as seen in *En attendant Godot* and its role in his total world view. Nevertheless, it may be interesting to point out to the reader in passing that while Edith Kern finds involuntary memory to be present in both Proust and Beckett, she notes that in Proust recollections have a beginning, a middle and an end, whereas in Beckett they are "absurd snatches of life." (Edith Kern, "Beckett's Knight of Infinite Resignation," *Yale French Studies: The New Dramatists* [vol. 29, 1962], p. 52.)

6. The cross-purpose positions described in this passage remind one of Mr. and Mrs. Rooney of *All That Fall*. "The perfect pair," says Mr. Rooney, "Like Dante's damned with their faces arsy-versy. Our tears will water our bottoms." *Krapp's Last Tape and Other Dramatic Pieces* (New York: Grove Press, 1957), p. 75.

7. We recognize the possibility that one could know of Jesus without knowing that he is "the Saviour." In this event, Estragon is revealing his unconcern with the problem of salvation, as he also does in not being able to remember that they are waiting for Godot, who is a "savior." The salvation theme of *En attendant Godot* will be discussed elsewhere in this chapter, and in Chapter Three.

8. Virtually every aspect of memory discussed here can be found in practically every work of Beckett, dramatic and otherwise. See especially *Krapp's Last Tape, Molloy, Malone Dies, All That Fall, Endgame*.

9. Compare also Estragon's "Nothing is sure" ("Rien n'est sûr" [p. 63]). Vladimir's refusal to listen to Estragon's dreams may be a precaution to avoid having to contend with any irrationality which would challenge his rational orientation.

10. See Cohn, "Philosophical Fragments," in Esslin (op. cit.), p. 171, where she says the name Didi can represent "Dis, Dis." She might have added that Gogo suggests the word *gogo*, a dupe, or else *à gogo*, the pleasure principle. Also see Bernard Dukore, "Gogo, Didi and the Absent Godot," *Drama Survey*, I, no. 2 (1962), where he argues that "Didi" and "Gogo" stand for "Id" and "Ego" (pp. 302–03). Dukore speculates further on the other names appearing in this play, and while these may be useful they are not pertinent to our study.

11. The problem arises as to whether Vladimir previously knew the pair Pozzo and Lucky, and this will be discussed in a later section of the chapter

dealing with recognition. Pozzo does refer to Lucky by name in Act II, p. 102.

12. Confusion concerning names is also a source of comedy, as in Pozzo's "Godet, Godot, Godin" (p. 33), and in his "Godin, Godet, Godot" (p. 42), as well as in the humorous variations on the name Pozzo with Estragon's "Bozzo" and Vladimir's "Gozzo" (p. 26).

13. It has already been noted in Chapter One that the floating proper nouns in the play have the additional effect of universalizing the characters. The names when taken as a whole present a composite and cosmopolitan picture of man in his history and in his geography.

14. Samuel Beckett, *Proust*, p. 8.

15. As has been seen in Chapter One and pointed out by various critics, the relationship between Vladimir and Estragon may be construed as having homosexual overtones. To the extent that this is the case, there is a certain loss of sexual identity present in the play. Fusion of sexual differentiation appears in other works of Beckett, especially in the famous trilogy. See in particular *Molloy* (New York: Grove Press, 1959), pp. 72–75.

16. Their roles appear to be a commentary on the haphazard nature of fate.

17. The majority of these themes dealing with identity appear in almost all the prose works and dramatic pieces of Beckett.

18. Indeed there may be some reason to argue that the interchangeable hats and shoes are symbolic of interchangeable identities. This may also be said of the passage in which Vladimir proposes to play at being Pozzo while Estragon imitates Lucky (p. 83).

19. It is frequently asserted that there may be some connection between Beckett's play and Balzac's *Mercadet*. See, for example, Brée's introduction to *En attendant Godot*, p. 6; see also Harry L. Butler's article, "Balzac and Godeau, Beckett and Godot: A Curious Parallel," *Romance Notes*, III, No. 2 (Spring, 1962), pp. 13–17. However, the fact that in Balzac's play the awaited Godeau arrives throws the analogy with *Mercadet* rather seriously off. Furthermore, having the action revolve around a figure who never appears on stage is an ancient theatrical device. Compare, for instance, Racine's *Andromaque*, in which the action revolves around the small boy, Astyanax. We learn from Hugh Kenner in "The Cartesian Centaur" (Esslin, op. cit., pp. 52–61) that Godeau is also the name of a real cyclist who represents close coordination of body and mind, which, as we have seen in Chapter One, the characters in the play do not have and probably can never achieve.

20. This passage is not present in the English version. However, its absence does not appear to us to alter our interpretation of Godot.

21. The locus of the play which in and of itself is vague will be discussed in the following chapter.

22. See especially C. Chadwick, "*Waiting for Godot:* A Logical Approach," *Symposium*, Vol. XIV, no. 4 (Winter, 1960), pp. 252–57.

23. This cannot apply to Pozzo and Lucky without adding the qualification that insofar as Pozzo is blind and Lucky mute in Act II it is conceivable that without Pozzo's vision and Lucky's voice—the prerequisites for recognition—another person could be substituted for Lucky.

24. Wylie Sypher, *Loss of the Self* (New York: Random House, 1962), p. 156. Beckett's most fully developed statement of this theme is found in *Film*.

Chapter 3

1. See p. 14 where Vladimir says to Estragon during the discussion of the Gospels, "Voyons, Gogo, il faut me renvoyer la balle de temps en temps." In English: "Come on, Gogo, return the ball, can't you, once in a way?" (p. 9).

2. If when Lucky describes God as having aphasia he means that this is an eternal condition, then his speech echoes Vladimir's doubt as to whether God has spoken to man through Scripture.

3. Beckett, *Proust*, p. 16.

4. Ibid., p. 9.

5. Ibid., p. 16.

6. Compare Pozzo: "Je n'arrive pas . . . à partir." Estragon: "C'est la vie" (p. 56). In English: Pozzo: "I don't seem to be able . . . to depart." Estragon: "Such is life" (p. 31).

7. See pp. 19–20 where they argue about which one of them will commit suicide first, and finally decide it will be more prudent to do nothing. The problem of suicide in the play will be treated in Chapter Five.

8. The themes of tedium and boredom are to be found in most of Beckett's works. See, for example, p. 348 of *Malone Dies* (New York: Grove Press, 1959).

9. For a more complete statement of Beckett on the relationship between life and the game see *Malone Dies*, pp. 265–66.

10. These linguistic games will be discussed in detail in Chapter Four of this study.

11. Although Estragon sleeps at other times during the play, this passage is especially significant because it comes after several frustrated attempts to find things to do.

12. See Beckett's commentary on Proust's conception of friendship as a function of man's cowardice and as the abortive negation of what is in

reality the irremediable solitude to which every human being is condemned, a conception which Beckett seems to share (*Proust*, p. 46).

13. Josephine Jacobsen and William R. Mueller, *The Testament of Beckett* (New York: Hill and Wang, 1964), p. 137.

14. In the French text Pozzo is not merely taking Lucky to the fair, but,
ironically enough, to the fair of Saint-Sauveur.

15. Eric Bentley, "The Talent of Samuel Beckett" in Cohn's *Casebook*,
op. cit., pp. 65–66. "A lot of comment on Beckett goes wrong in taking for
granted a pessimism more absolute than *Godot* embodies, in other words
in taking for granted that Godot will not come. This philosophical mistake
produces a mistake in dramatic criticism, for to remove the element of uncertainty and suspense is to remove an essential tension—in fact the essential drama." Contrast Gabor Mihalyi's statement in "Beckett's 'Godot'
and the Myth of Alienation," *Modern Drama*, vol. 9, no. 3 (December,
1966), also made regarding the dramatic structure of the play: "It is inevitable that Godot will never come, and it is no less inevitable that the
tramps will continue to await him" (p. 279).

16. Compare Beckett's *Act Without Words I* where instruments of salvation and egress are always just out of reach.

17. Pozzo states that the immediate future of Vladimir and Estragon
depends upon Godot (p. 33). It is only in the sense that Godot does not
arrive that he determines their future: their barren and tedious existences
must continue unchanged.

18. See *Act Without Words II* where one of the characters consults his
watch innumerable times in a matter of mere moments.

19. To this may be added the statement of Vladimir, "Déjà le temps
coule tout autrement. Le soleil se couchera, la lune se lèvera et nous partirons—d'ici" (p. 89). In English: "Time flows again already. The sun will
set, the moon rise, and we away . . . from here" (p. 50).

20. The characters show loss of consciousness of passage of time (p. 108).
The crepuscular atmosphere is reflected in Pozzo's description of the sky
(p. 43).

21. The English version of the play, in spite of references to Ireland and
England in Lucky's speech, shows the locale to be vaguely France. The
changes which have been made from one place to another in France can
be accounted for by the fact that they would be more readily recognized
by an English-speaking audience.

Chapter 4

1. The central argument of Michael Butler's "The Anatomy of Despair,"
Encore, vol. VIII, no. 3 (May–June, 1961), pp. 17–24 pertains to this failure
of communication.

2. While having no debt to Jerome Ashmore's article, "Philosophical Aspects of *Godot*," *Symposium*, vol. XVI, no. 4 (Winter, 1962), pp. 296–306, we wish to indicate that we are generally in agreement with his tenets regarding human discourse as well as other philosophical problems present in the play (skepticism, memory, time, etc.). However, we would suggest that ours is a more elaborate development of certain theses found in that article and more especially that we are in profound disagreement with his ideas concerning art in *Godot*, as will be seen in Chapter Six.

3. For a rather complete analysis of Lucky's speech see Anselm Atkins' article, "Lucky's Speech in Beckett's *Waiting for Godot:* A Punctuated Sense-Line Agreement," *Educational Theatre*, 19 (1967), pp. 426–32. This article, however, is restricted to the English language version, while we are concerned here primarily with the French version. However, let us note that the stuttering and stammering in Lucky's speech occur in both versions of the play, though not always in the same places.

4. Thus the father-son relationship discussed in Chapter One of this study appears in this instance to be reversed.

5. Note that the clarification contains within it the intellectual's approach to a problem; one avoids exposing oneself!

6. In English, "Pull on your trousers," which Estragon misunderstands as "pull off" (p. 60A).

7. It is important to note that in the former citation (p. 91) Vladimir ends his monologue with the question "Qu'en dis-tu?" ("What do you say to that?") to which Estragon replies "Je n'ai pas écouté" ("I wasn't listening"). Part of the failure to communicate lies with the person who is being addressed. The English passage (p. 51) differs radically here.

8. Ruby Cohn, "Philosophical Fragments" in Esslin (op. cit.), p. 171.

9. The English version of this passage (p. 52B) does not demonstrate this partial disintegration, as Pozzo says nothing. In the French version cited here Vladimir and Estragon are talking about leaving and Pozzo interrupts with a monetary offer of three and then four hundred (francs).

10. See Wolfgang Iser, "Samuel Beckett's Dramatic Language," *Modern Drama*, vol. 9, no. 3 (December, 1966), p. 255.

11.
Estragon: If I could only sleep.
Vladimir: Yesterday you slept.
Estragon: I'll try.
He resumes his foetal posture, his head between his knees.
Vladimir: Wait. (*He goes over and sits down beside Estragon and begins to sing in a loud voice.*)
Bye bye bye bye
Bye bye—

Estragon: (looking up angrily). Not so loud!
Vladimir: (softly).   Bye bye bye bye
                         Bye bye bye bye
                         Bye bye bye bye
                         Bye bye . . . (p. 45)

12. The passage obviously shows Pozzo's desperate need for company (already discussed in Chapter One), which makes parting with Estragon and Vladimir difficult. We may point out also the evidence here of speech that says one thing while gestures another; i.e., here is an example of stasis somewhat similar to the kind found at the end of each act. Nor should we overlook the traditional materials of comedy in this scene. Compare, for instance, Molière's satire of "precious manners," especially the scene in *La Comtesse d'Escarbagnas* in which the countess and Julie go through all sorts of contortions as to which of them will seat herself first. Molière, *Oeuvres complètes,* ed. Maurice Rat (Paris, 1956), II, pp. 727–28.

13. The comparison to Molière made in the preceding footnote applies equally well to this exchange between Vladimir and Estragon. Note that in the English version of this passage insults are present which do not occur in the French.

14. Compare the following passage from the English version which illustrates the use of rhyme and rhythm in the vaudeville routines:

Vladimir: We could do our exercises.
Estragon: Our movements.
Vladimir: Our elevations.
Estragon: Our relaxations.
Vladimir: Our elongations.
Estragon: Our relaxations. (p. 49)

15. One might compare the cycle of alimentation and elimination so often found in Beckett's works and referred to in the very center of Lucky's speech to the cycle of silence (alimentation) and speech (elimination) occurring in *En attendant Godot* and other works. The fact that Becket has composed two *actes sans paroles* also has bearing on this theme, just as Winnie's monologue in *Happy Days* bears on our discussion of the monologue in *En attendant Godot.*

16. For further ideas on the role of silence as well as of gesture and speech in Beckett see Atkins, op. cit.; J.-J. Mayoux, "Beckett and Expressionsm," *Modern Drama,* vol. 9, no. 3 (December, 1966), pp. 238–41; and his "Samuel Beckett and Universal Parody," in Esslin, op. cit. See also Ihab Hassan, *The Literature of Silence: Henry Miller and Samuel Beckett* (New York: Alfred A. Knopf, 1967).

17. Although there are those who might argue that to demonstrate the failure of reason and language is to signal the virtues of the non-rational,

it is our conviction that Beckett would see no more value in the non-rational aspects of man's existence than in the rational. It is hoped that the statements made in the preceding chapters together with those yet to be made will serve to support this view.

18. Stanley Rosen, *Nihilism* (New Haven: Yale University Press, 1969). See especially pp. xix, 6, 29, 37.

Chapter 5

1. Pp. 10–11, suicide is discussed; p. 13, reference is made to the Dead Sea; also, p. 13, reference is made to the crucifixion; p. 14, a distinction is made between death and hell; p. 15, it is suggested that the tree must be dead as it has no leaves.

2. Most of Beckett's characters are senile, and are often on the verge of death. See *Molloy, Malone Dies, Krapp's Last Tape, Endgame, Happy Days.*

3. P. 27, he is called carrion ("charogne") by Pozzo; p. 30, he is said to be "caving in" ("en train de crever") by Estragon; p. 30, his eyes are bulging out; p. 31, he refuses the bones for the first time; p. 47, Estragon suggests that his dance is called "La Mort du Lampiste"; p. 90, he sleeps a great deal, giving Vladimir and Estragon the impression that he is dead. In Act I he has lost the ability to speak coherently, and in Act II he is mute, which can be construed as marks of senility.

4. Marissel, *Beckett*, pp. 68–69: " . . . les bourreaux et les victimes se comptent par millions et se multiplient sans cesse. La plus profonde nécessité l'exige." [" . . . hangmen and victims can be found by the millions and ceaselessly increase. The profoundest necessity calls for it."]

5. Note Pozzo's "he's killing me" ("il m'assassine," [p. 39, l. 30]), said to draw to himself Vladimir's sympathy for Lucky. Pozzo's choice of words here is pertinent to our discussion, but his motivation in saying it is not pure.

6. This theme has important forebears in the history of literature and in the history of thought, especially as it is found in the works of Baudelaire and of Joseph de Maistre, both of whom develop the concept of the "Héautontimorouménos" (the hangman of oneself).

7. See Brée, p. 5; also compare scenes where the *suicide raté*—that is, suicide that is attempted unsuccessfully—occurs in Jean Louis Barrault's film about the mime, *Les Enfants du Paradis.* The device is also found in slapstick and black comedy, but the theme of silence in *Godot* seems to tie the *suicide raté* most closely to the traditional French mime.

8. Marissel discusses the possible objection we may have to the continuance of the characters in preference to suicide, saying, "Toujours très lu-

134   Notes

cide, Samuel Beckett a prévu cette objection. Vous ne le prendrez pas en défaut; cet écrivain est un logicien implacable. ' . . . Pour vous faire entrevoir, dit-il, jusqu'où allait la confusion de mes idées sur la mort, je vous dirai franchement que je n'excluais pas la possibilité qu'elle fût encore pire que la vie, en tant que condition. Je trouvais donc normal de ne pas m'y précipiter et, quand je m'oubliais au point de m'y essayer, de m'arrêter à temps.' " And a bit further on, " 'En ce qui me concerne personnellement, j'ai toujours préféré l'esclavage à la mort.' " ["Always very lucid, Samuel Beckett has foreseen this objection. You'll not catch him lacking; this writer is an implacable logician. 'To let you see,' he says, 'how far the confusion in my ideas on death went, I shall tell you frankly that I didn't exclude the possibility that it might be still worse than life, as far as a condition. Thus, I found it normal not to rush into it, and when I forgot myself to the point of trying it out, to stop in time. . . . As for my own personal concerns, I have always preferred slavery to death.' "] Marissel, op. cit., p. 68. See also Guicharnaud on suicide, op. cit., p. 240.

9.   Allen Brick, "A Note on Perception and Communication in Beckett's *Endgame*," *Modern Drama*, vol. 4, no. 1 (May, 1961), p. 21. Brick's argument is not without merit. There may be reason to say that Vladimir and Estragon do not commit suicide because if one or the other were left behind he would be in the position of having to restructure his habits. In other words, as we have frequently said, they stay together through habit.

10.   See Jacobsen and Mueller, op. cit., p. 8, where they contend that the hypothetical imperative of Beckett's characters is: *continue*. The idea is found in many critical essays, as it is a theme unquestionably found in the work of Beckett. See also in Jacobsen and Mueller, op. cit., a discussion of suicide, p. 31.

11.   Kenneth Hamilton's "Negative Salvation in Samuel Beckett," *Queen's Quarterly*, LXIX, no. 1 (Spring, 1962), pp. 102–11, presents an excellent picture of Beckett's religious outlook.

12.   Other vestiges of a Christian upbringing or orientation come in Vladimir's speech, notably in the passage where he says, "The last moment is long, but it will be good. Who said that?" (p. 11), which is a quotation from the Bible, but one he is unable to trace, as can be seen from the context. Estragon's use of the names Cain and Abel, whom he refers to as "toute l'humanité" (p. 96), indicates some kind of religious background in his case, too, despite the fact that he does not remember whether he went to a parochial school or not (p. 13). Furthermore, on a more profound level Vladimir seems to have intimations of a being—which for no reason should be identified with Godot—who watches over him as he sleeps (p. 106). Whether this is an indication of mere vestiges of his upbringing or of his real belief is altogether moot, however.

13. Eva Metman discusses this reversal of Matthew 25, 33 in her article "Reflections on Samuel Beckett's Plays" found in Esslin, op. cit., pp. 125, 129.

14. See in particular Hélène L. Webner's "*Waiting for Godot* and the New Theology," *Renascence*, vol. 21, no. 1, pp. 3–9, 31.

15. Compare the ladder imagery in *Endgame* which perhaps ironically refers to Jacob's ladder. Also in *Watt* ("Do not come down the ladder, I have taken it away.") See in this connection Thomas Hogan's "The Reversed Metamorphosis" in *Irish Writing*, no. 26 (March, 1954), p. 62: " 'Don't come down the ladder, I have taken it away.' The old joke (which Mr. Beckett uses twice) is a useful warning." Hogan applies the concept to any elaborate superstructure of interpretation.

16. See such passages as those in which he confesses that he is not very human (p. 33, ll. 12–13); or in which he boasts of goodness, which represents a salving of conscience, (pp. 36–37); or of his generosity (p. 45, ll. 28–29). Michael Butler, op. cit., p. 20 ff., speaks of Pozzo's "intermittent conscience." In our opinion it is more insincere than it is intermittent.

17. See Bernard Dukore's "Gogo, Didi and the Absent Godot," op. cit., where he argues that Vladimir and Estragon have no superego, hence no moral sense. This concept may stem from what we consider to be not so much an absence of morality as confused and disintegrating morality.

18. "Let us do something, while we have the chance! It is not every day that we are needed. Not indeed that we personally are needed. Others would meet the case equally well, if not better" (p. 51).

19. See Dennis Douglas, "The Drama of Evasion in *Waiting for Godot*," *Komos*, vol. 1, no. 4 (1968), p. 141.

20. Samuel Beckett, "Dante . . . Bruno. Vico . . Joyce," *transition*, 16–17 (June, 1929), p. 253.

21. Vladimir recognizes that action is deferred by the (difficult) need to make a decision (p. 73).

22. See Holden, p. 58, regarding Beckett's view of the will.

23. See especially Douglas, op. cit., p. 142.

24. The egoism fundamental to each of the characters makes Rexroth's assertion that the dignity of the tramps lies in the comradeship of their waiting improbable. Kenneth Rexroth, "The Point of Irrelevance," *The Nation*, CLXXXII, no. 15 (Apr. 14, 1956), p. 328. Likewise, Edith Kern's assertion that "Beckett's characters in this play glorify . . . the all-surpassing power of human tenderness which alone makes bearable man's long and ultimately futile wait for a redeemer and which, in fact, turns out itself to be the redeemer of man in his forlornness" (p. 47), seems inaccurate. Not only the respective egoism of the two men but also the ambivalence we have seen in this relationship preclude building much of a case on the

redemptive power of tenderness. Edith Kern, "Drama Stripped for Inaction," *Yale French Studies*, Vol. 14 (1954–55), pp. 41–47.

25. John Gruen, "Samuel Beckett Talks about Samuel Beckett," *Vogue* (December, 1969), p. 210. In this article Beckett is quoted as saying that every man must know that " 'self-perception is the most frightening of all human observations. He must know that when man faces himself, he is looking into the abyss.' " This is the theme Beckett explores in *Film*.

26. Beckett in "Letters on 'Endgame'," *The Village Voice* (Mar. 19, 1958), pp. 8, 15.

27. See a discussion of silence in Wittgenstein and Heidegger by Stanley Rosen, loc. cit., p. 133.

28. Among others, Bentley, loc. cit. and Donald Davie, "Kinds of Comedy," *Spectrum*, Vol. 2, no. 1 (Winter, 1958), p. 27.

29. G. E. Wellworth, "Life in the Void: Samuel Beckett," *University [of Kansas City] Review*, vol. XXVIII (1961), p. 33: "Beckett is the prophet of negation and sterility. He holds out no hope to humanity, only a picture of unrelieved blackness; and those who profess to see in Beckett signs of a Christian approach or signs of compassion are simply refusing to see what is there."

30. Compare the statement of Pierre Aimé Touchard, in "Un Théâtre nouveau," *Avant Scène*, no. 156 (1957), p. 2: "Beckett condamne la Vie même qui n'est qu'une attente sans intérêt, sans foi et sans amour de la mort. Pour lui, l'existence ne se justifie en somme que par son aboutissement fatal: le Néant." In English: "Beckett condemns Life itself which is nothing but a wait without interest, without faith, without love for death. For him, existence is justified in short only by its fatal ending: Nothingness."

31. Huguette Delye, *Samuel Beckett ou la Philosophie de l'absurde* (Aix-en-Provence: La Pensée Universitaire, 1960), p. 75.

Chapter 6

1. William Thompson, "Freedom and Comedy," *Tulane Drama Review*, vol. IX, no. 3 (Spring 1965), p. 230.

2. Samuel Beckett, *Watt* (New York: Grove Press, 1959), p. 48.

3. See the play, p. 67, l. 6: "Vladimir suspend son vol." ["Vladimir suspends his flight."] Brée says of this that it is a "humorously grandiloquent expression" for "Vladimir stops," echoing, of course, Lamartine's "Le Lac." What is interesting in this is that the humor can be appreciated only by the reader, since it is a stage direction.

4. Henri Bergson, "Laughter," in *Comedy*, ed. Wylie Sypher (New York: Doubleday, 1956), p. 64.

5. There are, of course, the three-syllable names Estragon and Vladimir in the written text, and the name Vladimir does appear in the dialogue.

6. For the lyrical we have Pozzo on time (p. 104) and Pozzo on the night (p. 43). For the rhetorical we have Vladimir trying to persuade Estragon— as well as himself—that they should help Pozzo get up (p. 91). There are also mixtures of these elements, or else of the lyrical and the conversational, within the same speech, notably Vladimir's musing over the sleeping Estragon (p. 105). It is difficult to separate the rhetorical from the lyrical in the case of Pozzo. Vladimir's Latin quotation concerning memory of past happiness (p. 99) may also be regarded as emanating from a rhetorical tradition. Fragments of the rhetorical and lyrical can be seen in Lucky's speech, where remnants of the style of persuasion ("Etant donné l'existence telle qu'elle jaillit des récents travaux publics de Poinçon et Wattmann d'un Dieu personnel . . . " [p. 51]) coincide with poetic fragments ("si bleues . . . si calmes" [p. 51], repeated on p. 53), which are, of course, from Verlaine's "Le Ciel est par-dessus le toit . . . " In the English version (28B) the persuasive tradition is definitely felt when Lucky says, "Given the existence as uttered forth in the public works of Puncher and Wattmann of a personal God . . . " The poetry of the words "so blue still and calm so calm . . . " is not so conspicuous unless the English reader happens to be familiar with the famous French poem of Verlaine.

7. See John Sheedy in "The Net," Casebook, op. cit., pp. 160–65. Although Sheedy does not elaborate upon this, it is not difficult to see that Estragon's personality has a greater impact than Vladimir's in Act I, where furthermore there is a greater amount of gross physical comedy, while in Act II we find Vladimir manipulating Estragon more than in Act I and delivering rather extensive monologues on duty and on life and death.

8. Ruby Cohn, "The Absurdly Absurd: Avatars of Godot," Comparative Literature Studies, vol. 21 (1965), p. 240.

9. Allen Thiher, "Le Maître de Santiago and Tragic Affirmation," Romance Notes, vol. XI, no. 2 (Winter 1969), pp. 238–43. One might say the same for Eugene O'Neill (Mourning Becomes Electra) or for yet another nihilist, Robinson Jeffers (Medea).

10. Jean Anouilh, Antigone (Paris: La Table Ronde, 1947), pp. 38–39. The Chorus presents a theory of tragedy in this passage.

11. Thus, we would admit—at least in part—Raymond Williams' thesis found in Modern Tragedy (Stanford: Stanford University Press, 1966) that we have here an example of the tragedy of the total condition of man (p. 153), as well as a tragic rhythm in the inseparability or interlocked illusions of Estragon and Vladimir, who remain together in spite of the stalemate in which they find themselves (p. 155). We may regard this stalemate as

a ramification of the stasis we have already observed in all four characters of the play. According to Williams, "In a stalemate, there is no possibility of movement or even the effort at movement; every willed action is self-cancelling" (p. 142).

12. See Pierre Yerlès, "Le Théâtre de Samuel Beckett," *La Revue Nouvelle*, vol. 33, no. 4 (April 1961), p. 402, where he refers to "this paralysis of the will" and to "leurs simulacres de volonté" which, he says, "n'existent qu'au niveau de langage" (i.e., "their semblances of will which exist only at the linguistic level"). See also p. 403, where he writes that the "sous-hommes" (sub-men) of Beckett are motivated by conditioned reflexes." Compare João Mendes, who writes in his "Vida Literária," *Brotéria*, vol. 69 (1959), p. 60, that Lucky and Pozzo are "autómatos" or automatons.

13. Isolationism is described by Thompson, op. cit., as follows: "The farce, the comedy, the absurd drama: what we are really talking about with all these genres is simply the anthropology of values: the difference in values of a community, a civilization and a collective. The hero of the farce demands that the universe be changed; the hero of the comedy demands that society accommodate itself to his will; the absurd hero makes no demands: the universe is beyond mere belief and society is incorrigibly a hoax. The absurd hero withdraws into himself, or rather he makes a gesture of his self: the infinite expressions of the human face gain the exact freedom of an immovable absurd mask" (p. 230).

14. Edith Hamilton, *The Greek Way to Western Civilization* (New York: Mentor), p. 169: "Tragedy's preoccupation is with suffering. . . . There is no dignity like the dignity of a soul in agony."

15. "The tears of the world are a constant quantity. For each one who begins to weep somewhere else another stops. The same is true of the laugh" (p. 22).

16. Geoffrey Brereton, *Principles of Tragedy* (Coral Gables, Fla.: University of Miami Press, 1968), p. 250: "Vladimir's exclamation of horror stems from the obvious truth that a twentieth-century mentality can derive little comfort from the image of an Old Testament-type God. The kind of salvation which a white-bearded Godot is likely to offer will hardly satisfy even Vladimir and Estragon, impoverished though they are. From the religious point of view, strongly implicit in the play, *Waiting for Godot* might well have been subtitled 'Nobodaddy's Revenge'." But the conversation in the play is, as we have seen, so chaotic, that Brereton may well be reading too much into Vladimir's ejaculation, which could be a mere speech habit, void of religious meaning.

17. Tom Driver, "Beckett by the Madeleine," in *Columbia University Forum Anthology* (New York: Atheneum, 1968), p. 128.

18. Beckett, *Proust*, p. 49.

19. Ibid., p. 29.

20. Thus Janvier's argument for an optimistic tragedy based on the tranquillity or courage of the characters vis-à-vis their situation seems to overlook their fundamental superficiality, that is their willful blindness to the real source of their ills. Ludovic Janvier, *Pour Samuel Beckett* (Paris: Les Editions de Minuit, 1966), pp. 103–04.

21. Beckett, *Watt*, loc. cit. Also compare the dialogue concerning laughter from *Fin de Partie* (Paris: Editions de Minuit, 1957), pp. 33–34. Note also the role of laughter in Beckett's *Play* (London: Faber and Faber, Ltd., 1964), p. 21.

22. See Jacobsen and Mueller, op. cit., p. 79: "Beckett's comedy, though it has its lighter moments, consummately executed, is for the most part a devastating howl of pain, evoked by contemplation of the human condition."

23. This would not apply to any significant extent to the sentimental comedy, which, anyway, is not present in *En attendant Godot* under any circumstances.

24. Beckett, *Proust*, p. 16.

25. One might also ask why Beckett writes in French. We have found no better answer to this question than the one provided by Janvier which contends that it is a matter of cultural mutation, self-discipline and self-punishment, and which concludes with the following assertions: "Or, l'écrivain a pris soin d'indiquer que le choix du français était pour lui une sorte de pari, tout simplement, en disant un jour, comme le plus banalement possible afin de décourager les enquêteurs, que ce n'était plus du tout la même chose d'écrire dans cette langue toute neuve car, insistait-il 'it was more exciting for me, writing in French'. Dans cet aveu fort plat et 'dépouillé d'artifice', nous voyons pour notre part, serait-ce avec de trop bons yeux, le pari de renouvellement et le risque de la renaissance." Janvier, op. cit., p. 225. ("Now, the writer has taken care to indicate that the choice of French for him was a sort of game, simply by saying one day, in the most banal fashion possible, in order to discourage the curious, that it was no longer the same thing at all to write in this brand new language, for, he insisted, 'it was more exciting for me, writing in French.' In this very flat confession, and one 'stripped of artifice', we for our part see, even if too favorably, the bet of renewal and the risk of renaissance.")

26. Beckett himself appears to endorse the concept of diversion when he argues that the pleasure of the viewer (or reader?) is a justification for

140   Notes

the existence of an art object at least on a public level. Note that Lawrence
E. Harvey in his book *Samuel Beckett: Poet and Critic* (Princeton, N.J.:
Princeton University Press) writes " . . . *plaire* in his [Beckett's] view takes
radical precedence over *instruire*" (p. 431). As the reader will see in the
remainder of our chapter, the picture is perhaps more complicated than
Harvey's statement would suggest.

27. Beckett, *Proust*, p. 47. Compare from Beckett's "La Peinture des
Van Velde," *Les Cahiers d'Art*, vol. 20–21 (1945–1946), pp. 349–56, the
following assertion: "Avec les mots on ne fait que se raconter. Eux-mêmes
les lexicographes se déboutonnent. Et jusque dans le confessional on se
trahit" (p. 349). ("With words one only recounts oneself. The lexicographers
themselves open up. And one betrays oneself even in the confessional.")

28. Driver, loc. cit.

29. Mendes, op. cit., p. 61: " . . . esta peça significa alguma coisa, e
prova, contra o Autor, que a arte e a inteligência ao menos, não são ab-
surdas. Porque podem significar alguma coisa." ("This play means something, and proves, despite the Author, that art and intelligence at least are
not absurd. Because they can mean something.")

30. See Lawrence E. Harvey in *Configuration critique de Samuel Beckett*, ed. by M. J. Friedman (Paris: Minard, 1964), p. 166, where Beckett's
art is called an art of exorcism that diminishes the pain of living.

31. One of the major themes of *The Unnamable* is the compulsion to
speak brought into conflict with the desire for silence. See in particular in
this connection Samuel Beckett, *The Unnamable*, in the trilogy, *Molloy,
Malone Dies and The Unnamable* (New York: Grove Press, 1959), pp. 416–
17.

32. Beckett, *Proust*, p. 47. See also Beckett's "Three Dialogues," *transition*, no. 5 (1949), pp. 101 and 103, where he speaks of Bram Van Velde's
obligation to act and to paint, however unable he is to act and to paint.

33. Beckett, *Proust*, p. 8: "Or rather life is a succession of habits, since
the individual is a succession of individuals . . ."

34. Jerome Ashmore, op. cit., pp. 296–97: "The range of Beckett's devastating account of the human predicament includes the fields of politics,
economics, theology, society, education, metaphysics, discourse, physical
science, and history. Each one of them is found defective when viewed in
the light of its bearing on existence considered intrinsically. Fine art escapes Beckett's negating eye but only by omission. Absence of reference
to it spares it from exhibition as one more endeavor that has failed to contribute existentially to human welfare."

35. Beckett, *Proust*, p. 16.

36. Ibid.

37. See Driver, loc. cit., where Beckett speaks of our chance of renovation.

38. Playing at being Lucky and Pozzo is a suspension of the usual or habitual means of passing time—and thus it is an attempt to be artistic. But it is a thing which soon fails, partly because it cannot be sustained (boredom quickly enters in), and partly because it is generated from the basic habit of wanting to do nothing except fill in time, rather than from some more profound artistic intention. Much the same sort of comment could be made of Vladimir's use of music, when he sings a round to himself to pass the time, to combat his solitude, to contend with silence.

39. It should not be construed that, when the ego-centered Estragon says this, he is referring to anything except his own particular plight. He is not concerned with the "mess" Beckett speaks of, which is universal in scope. The individual members of the audience, too, are enmeshed in their own ego-oriented problems, and so are unable to address themselves to the larger and more profound (because universal) predicament of the human condition.

40. Philip Stratford, "Creativity and Commitment in Contemporary Theater," *Humanities Association of Canada Bulletin*, vol. 15, no. 2 (Autumn, 1964), p. 39.

41. Stanley R. Hopper, "Irony—the Pathos of the Middle," *Cross Currents*, vol. 12, no. 1 (Winter 1962), p. 35: "First of all, the ironist enjoys a temporary advantage over the problem, his subject matter. By specifying the discord, the discrepancy, aesthetically, he presides over it and thus exempts himself from the ethical requirement (that he do something about it)."

42. Driver, loc. cit.

43. In Lionel Gossman, *Men and Masks* (Baltimore: The Johns Hopkins Press, 1963), p. 303.

Chapter 7

1. Gustav E. Mueller, "Philosophy in the Twentieth Century American Novel," *Journal of Aesthetics and Art Criticism*, vol. XVI, no. 4 (June 1958), p. 471.

2. G. J. Warnock, *English Philosophy Since 1900* (New York: Oxford University Press, 1966), p. 102.

3. Ibid., p. 108.

4. Aristotle, *On Poetry and Style* (New York: The Library of Liberal Arts, 1958), p. 7.

5. Stephen D. Ross, *Literature and Philosophy* (New York: Appleton-Century-Crofts, 1969), pp. 19, 58.

6. Mueller, op cit., p. 471.

7. Henri Bergson, *An Introduction to Metaphysics* (Indianapolis: The Library of Liberal Arts, 1949), pp. 21–24.

8. As we have demonstrated in Chapter One, it is Pozzo and Lucky who embody cruel fraternity, while Estragon and Vladimir represent ambivalent fraternity.

9. See in this connection Camus's *La Peste* or Teilhard de Chardin's *L'Avenir de l'homme* (Paris: Editions du Seuil, 1959), pp. 179–87.

10. John Fletcher, op. cit., p. 126 ff. We are of course not concerned here or elsewhere in this book with the "influence" of any given philosopher such as Heidegger or Geulincx on Beckett's world view, but, rather and only in passing, with the similarities and differences between Beckett's nihilistic skepticism and that of others. For this reason we have not entered into a discussion of Wittgenstein and Beckett, there not being in our opinion a noteworthy connection, except in their concepts of language and silence which have been mentioned in Chapter 4.

11. Ibid., pp. 122–23. These philosophers are alluded to frequently in Beckett's work. Heraclitus figures in Estragon's "On ne descend pas deux fois dans le même pus" (p. 69), and both are suggested in Pozzo's statement on laughter and tears. Beckett's substitution of "pus" for river in the famous statement of Heraclitus shows his cynical view of life, and is another way of referring to the "merde universelle."

12. Albert Camus, *The Myth of Sisyphus* (New York: Vintage Books, 1960), p. v.

13. Ibid., p. 5.

14. Ibid., p. 91. As we have noted earlier, another source of optimism in Camus which is negated by Beckett is the efficacy of fruitful fraternity in the struggle against the absurd.

15. No more powerful statement on the powerlessness of language and the compulsion of the artist can be found than the following one by Beckett in one of his dialogues with Georges Duthuit: "The expression that there is nothing to express, nothing from which to express, no power to express, no desire to express, together with the obligation to express." The statement also embodies Beckett's nihilistic world view. Samuel Beckett, "Three Dialogues," *transition*, no. 5 (1949), p. 98. One might add to this exposure of the failure of language through the use of language the observation that in order to see how Beckett portrays the limitations of memory one must have a memory, just as Beckett himself must have a memory in order to show its deficiencies in his characters.

16. Dorothy Walsh, "The Cognitive Content of Art" in *The Problems of Aesthetics*, ed. E. Vivas and M. Krieger (New York: Holt, Rinehart & Winston, 1965), p. 609.

17. Amy Kleppner, "Philosophy and the Literary Medium: The Existentialist Predicament," *Journal of Aesthetics and Art Criticism*, vol. XXIII, no. 2 (Winter 1964), p. 210.

18. Ibid., p. 214.

19. Ross, op. cit., pp. 58, 213.

20. See John Hospers, "Implied Truths in Literature," *Journal of Aesthetics and Art Criticism*, vol. XIX, no. 1 (Fall 1960), pp. 37–46.

21. Driver, op. cit., p. 129.

22. Kleppner, op. cit., p. 108.

23. Lawrence W. Hyman, "Moral Values and the Literary Experience," *Journal of Aesthetics and Art Criticism*, vol. XXIV, no. 4 (Summer, 1966), p. 540.

24. The same desire to understand characterizes the writer or the reader of philosophy, thus giving us another point of similarity between the two domains.

25. See in this connection John F. Reichert, "Description and Interpretation in Literary Criticism," *Journal of Aesthetics and Art Criticism*, vol. XXVII, no. 3 (Spring, 1969), pp. 286–88.

26. Compare Morris Weitz, *Philosophy in Literature* (Detroit: Wayne State University, 1963). Judging from his analyses of *Candide, Anna Karenina, Hamlet* and *A La Recherche du temps perdu,* Weitz appears to assume that there is only one depth meaning for a given work of literature. This would suggest that there is only one valid interpretation of the work, at least in the realm of content, and since we have seen that form and content cannot be separated, he is in essence saying that there is only one valid interpretation.

27. Reichert, op. cit., p. 288.

28. Morris Weitz, *Philosophy of the Arts* (Cambridge: Harvard University Press, 1950). On p. 140 Weitz writes the following concerning *Native Son*: "It is only when one comes to discern this depth meaning that the novel takes on its basic significance. Until it becomes clear that Bigger is more than a symbol of exploitation and represents *all* men who struggle to realize themselves in a world full of evil, the novel remains a mere adequate proletarian one. But it is this meaning that gives the novel its universality."

BIBLIOGRAPHY OF
WORKS CONSULTED

Abirached, Robert. "Carnet de théâtre." *Etudes*, 310, No. 7–8 (July–August 1961), 131–34.

——. "Problèmes actuels du Théâtre Populaire." *Etudes*, 303 (Dec. 1959), 368–72.

——. "La Voix tragique de Samuel Beckett." *Etudes*, 320 (Jan. 1964), 85–88.

Anouilh, Jean. *Antigone*. Paris: La Table Ronde, 1947.

Aristotle. *On Poetry and Style*. New York: The Bobbs-Merrill Company, Inc. (The Library of Liberal Arts), 1958.

Ashmore, Jerome. "Philosophical Aspects of *Godot*." *Symposium*, 16, No. 4 (Winter 1962), 296–306.

Atkins, Anselm. "Lucky's Speech in Beckett's *Waiting for Godot*: A Punctuated Sense-Line Arrangement." *Educational Theatre Journal*, 19 (1967), 426–32.

Barjon, Louis. "Le Dieu de Beckett." *Etudes*, 323 (Dec. 1965), 650–62.

Beckett, Samuel. "Dante . . . Bruno. Vico . . Joyce." *transition*, 16–17 (June 1929), 242–53.

——. *En attendant Godot*. Ed. Germaine Brée. New York: The MacMillan Company, 1963.

——. *En attendant Godot* (alternate edition). New York: French and European Publication (Editions de Minuit), n. d.

——. *Endgame*, New York: Grove Press, Inc., 1958.

——. *Film* (original project). New York: Grove Press, Inc. (Evergreen).

——. *Fin de Partie*. Paris: Editions de Minuit, 1957.

——. *Krapp's Last Tape and other dramatic pieces*. New York: Grove Press, Inc., 1957. (Includes *All That Fall, Embers, Act Without Words I*, and *Act Without Words II*.)

————. *Molloy, Malone Dies, The Unnamable.* 1st ed. New York: Grove Press, Inc., 1959.

————. "La peinture des Van Velde." *Les Cahiers d'Art,* 20–21 (1945–1946), 349–56.

————. *Play and Two Short Pieces for Radio.* London: Faber & Faber, Ltd., 1964. (Also contains *Words and Music* and *Cascando.*)

————. *Proust.* New York: Grove Press, Inc., 1931.

————. *Waiting for Godot.* New York: Grove Press, Inc., 1954.

————. *Watt.* New York: Grove Press, Inc., 1959.

Beckett, Samuel, and Duthuit, George. "Three Dialogues." *transition,* no. 5 (1949), 97–103.

"Beckett on Proust." *The Times Literary Supplement,* No. 3331 (30 Dec. 1965), 1208.

"Beckett's Letters on 'Endgame'—Extracts from His Correspondence with Director Alan Schneider." *The Village Voice,* (19 Mar. 1958), 8, 15.

Bergson, Henri. *An Introduction to Metaphysics.* Indianapolis: The Library of Liberal Arts, 1949.

————. Laughter, in *Comedy.* Ed. Wylie Sypher. New York: Doubleday & Company, Inc., 1956.

————. *Matter and Memory.* London: Allen Unwin, 1911.

Bishop, Tom. "Samuel Beckett." *Saturday Review,* 15 Nov. 1969, 26–27 & 59.

Blanchot, Maurice. "Where now? Who now?" *Evergreen Review,* 2, No. 7 (Winter 1959), 222–29.

Blau, Herbert. "Meanwhile follow the bright angels." *Tulane Drama Review,* 5, No. 1 (Sept. 1960), 89–101.

————. "The Popular, the absurd, and the *entente cordiale.*" *Tulane Drama Review,* 5, No. 3 (Mar. 1961), 119–51.

Block-Michel, Jean. *Le présent de l'indicatif.* Paris: Gallimard, N. R. F., 1963.

Brick, Allan. "A Note on Perception and Communication in Beckett's *Endgame.*" *Modern Drama,* 4, No. 1 (May 1961), 20–22.

Brooks, Curtis. "The Mythic Pattern in *Waiting for Godot.*" *Modern Drama,* 9, No. 3 (Dec. 1966), 292–99.

Bryden, Ronald. "Second Non-Coming." *New Statesman,* 69, No. 1765 (8 Jan. 1965), 50–51.

Bull, Peter. "Waiting for God Knows What." *Plays and Players,* 3, No. 8 (May 1956), 7.

Burgess, Anthony. "The Universal Mess." *The Manchester Guardian,* 717, No. 36 (24 July 1964), 9.

Butler, Harry L. "Balzac and Godeau, Beckett and Godot: a curious parallel." *Romance Notes,* 3, No. 2 (Spring 1962), 13–17.

Butler, Michael. "Anatomy of Despair." *Encore*, 8, No. 3 (May–June 1961), 17–24.

Camus, Albert. *De l'Envers et l'endroit à l'exil et le royaume*. New York: Dell Publishing Co., Inc., 1963.

————. *The Myth of Sisyphus*. New York: Vintage Books (Random House, Inc.), 1960.

————. *La Peste*. New York: The Macmillan Co., 1947.

Castellano, José. "Lo Trágico en Beckett y Unamuno." *Punto Europa* (Madrid), Oct. 1963, 75–97.

Chadwick, C. "Waiting for Godot: A Logical Approach." *Symposium*, 14, No. 4 (Winter 1960), 252–57.

Chambers, Ross. "A Theatre of Dilemma and Myth." *Meanjin*, 25, No. 3 (1966), 306–17.

Champigny, Robert. "Interprétation de *En attendant Godot*." *PMLA*, 75, No. 3 (June 1960), 329–31.

Chatterjee, Margaret. "Some Philosophical Problems Arising in the Arts." *Journal of Aesthetics and Art Criticism*, 27, No. 3 (Spring 1969), 335–39.

Chiaromonte, Nicola. "La Predica di Beckett." *Il Mondo*, anno 16, No. 21 (26 May 1964), 17.

Coe, Richard. "God and Samuel Beckett." *Meanjin*, 24, No. 1 (1965), 66–85.

Cohn, Ruby. "The Absurdly Absurd: Avatars of Godot." *Comparative Literature Studies*, 21 (1965), 233–40.

————. "Philosophical Fragments in the Works of Samuel Beckett." *Criticism*, 6, No. 1 (Winter 1964), 33–43. (Also in Esslin, p. 169, ff.).

————. "Plays and Players in the Plays of Samuel Beckett." *Yale French Studies*, 29 (1962), 43–48.

————. *Samuel Beckett, the comic gamut*. New Brunswick: Rutgers University Press, 1962.

————, ed. *Casebook on Waiting for Godot*. New York: Grove Press, Inc., 1967.

Corrigan, Robert W. "The Image of Man in the Contemporary Theatre." *Forum*, 3, No. 2 (Spring 1959), 46–55.

————. "The Theatre in Search of a Fix." *Tulane Drama Review*, 5, No. 4 (June 1961), 21–35.

Damiens, Claude. "Regards sur le 'Théâtre Nouveau.'" *Paris Théâtre*, 14ᵉ année, No. 173 (1967), 12–13.

Davie, Donald. "Kinds of Comedy." *Spectrum*, 2, No. 1 (Winter 1958), 25–31.

Delye, Huguette. *Samuel Beckett ou la Philosophie de l'absurde*. Aix-en-

Provence: La Pensée Universitaire, 1960.

Donoghue, Denis. "The Play of Words." *The Listener*, XVIII, No. 1737 (12 July 1962), 55–57.

Douglas, Dennis. "The Drama of Evasion in *Waiting for Godot*." *Komos*, 1 (4) (1968), 140–46.

Driver, Tom F. "Beckett by the Madeleine." *Columbia University Forum Anthology*. New York: Atheneum Publishers, 1968.

Dukore, Bernard. "Gogo, Didi and the Absent Godot." *Drama Survey*, 1, No. 2 (1962), 301–07.

Dumur, Guy. "Les Métamorphoses du Théâtre d'Avant-Garde." *Théâtre populaire*, 2ᵉ Trimestre, No. 42 (1961), 100–06.

Esslin, Martin. *The Theatre of the Absurd*. Garden City, New York: Doubleday & Company, Inc. (Anchor Books), 1961.

————, ed. *Samuel Beckett, a Collection of Critical Essays*. Englewood Cliffs: Prentice-Hall, Inc., 1965.

Fanizza, Franco. *Letteratura come filosofia*. Manduria: Lacaita, 1963. See Chapter IV "La Parola e il silenzio ne *L'Innomable* di Samuel Beckett*," 63–73.

Feibleman, James K. "The Truth-Value of Art." *Journal of Aesthetics and Art Criticism*, 24, No. 4 (Summer 1966), 501–08.

Fletcher, John. *Samuel Beckett's Art*. London: Chatto & Windus, 1967.

Fowlie, Wallace. "The New French Theater." *Sewanee Review*, 67, No. 4 (Autumn 1959), 643–57.

Francis, Richard Lee. "Beckett's Metaphysical Tragicomedy." *Modern Drama*, 8, No. 3 (Dec. 1965), 259–67.

Friedman, Melvin. *Configuration critique de Samuel Beckett*. Paris: Minard, 1964.

————. "The Creative Writer as Polyglot." *The Wisconsin Academy of Sciences, Arts and Letters, Transactions*, 49 (1960), 229–36.

Gendin, Sidney. "The Artist's Intentions." *Journal of Aesthetics and Art Criticism*, 23, No. 2 (Winter 1964), 193–96.

Glicksberg, Charles I. *Modern Literature and the Death of God*. The Hague: Martinus Nijhoff, 1966.

————. *The Self in Modern Literature*. University Park: The Pennsylvania State University Press, 1963.

Goldstein, Harvey D. "Mimesis and Catharsis Reexamined." *Journal of Aesthetics and Art Criticism*, 24, No. 4 (Summer 1966), 567–77.

Gossman, Lionel. *Men and Masks*. Baltimore: The Johns Hopkins Press, 1963.

Grene, Marjorie. *Martin Heidegger*. New York: Hillary House, 1957

Gresset, Michel. "Comédie." *Mercure de France*, No. 1209–10 (July–Aug.

1964), 546–47.

Grossvogel, David I. *The Blasphemers*. Ithaca: Cornell University Press, 1962.

———. *The Self-Conscious Stage in Modern French Drama*. New York: Columbia University Press, 1958.

Gruen, John. "Samuel Beckett talks about Samuel Beckett." *Vogue* (Dec. 1969), 21.

Guicharnaud, Jacques. *Modern French Theatre from Giraudoux to Genêt*. New Haven: Yale University Press, 1967.

Gurmendez, Carlos. "Mendigos metafísicos; Beckett o la desesperación." *Indice de artes y letras* (Jan. 1964), 19–20.

Hamilton, Edith. *The Greek Way to Western Civilization*. New York: New American Library of World Literature (Mentor), n.d.

Hamilton, Kenneth. "Boon or Thorn? Joyce Cary and Samuel Beckett on Human Life." *The Dalhousie Review*, 38, No. 4 (Winter 1959), 433–42.

———. "Negative Salvation in Samuel Beckett." *Queen's Quarterly*, 69, No. 1 (Spring 1962), 102–11.

Harvey, Lawrence E. "Art and the Existential in *En attendant Godot*." *PMLA*, 75, No. 1 (Mar. 1960), 137–46.

———. "Samuel Beckett on Life, Art, and Criticism." *Modern Language Notes*, 80, No. 5 (Dec. 1965), 545–62.

———. *Samuel Beckett, Poet and Critic*. Princeton: Princeton University Press, 1970.

Hassan, Ihab. *The Literature of Silence: Henry Miller and Samuel Beckett*. New York: Alfred A. Knopf, Inc., 1967.

Hathaway, John. "Apuntes biográficos sobre Samuel Beckett." *índice* (Madrid), año 25, No. 257–58 (Nov. 1969), 46–47.

Heidegger, Martin. *An Introduction to Metaphysics*. Garden City, New York: Anchor Books (Doubleday & Co., Inc.), 1959.

———. *Being and Time*. New York: Harper & Row, 1962.

Hesla, David H. *The Shape of Chaos: an Interpretation of the Art of Samuel Beckett*. Minneapolis: The University of Minnesota Press, 1971.

Hoffman, Frederick J. *The Mortal No: Death and the Modern Imagination*. Princeton: Princeton University Press, 1964.

Hogan, Thomas. "The Reversed Metamorphosis." *Irish Writing*, No. 26 (Mar. 1954), 54–62.

Hopper, Stanley R. "Irony—the Pathos of the Middle." *Cross Currents*, 12, No. 1 (Winter 1962), 31–40.

Hornick, Henry. "On Change in Literature." *Journal of Aesthetics and Art Criticism*, 17, No. 3 (Mar. 1959), 330–43.

Hospers, John. "Implied Truths in Literature." *Journal of Aesthetics and*

Art Criticism, 19, No. 1 (Fall 1960), 37–46.

Hyman, Lawrence W. "Moral Values and the Literary Experience." *Journal of Aesthetics and Art Criticism*, 24, No. 4 (Summer 1966), 539–47.

Iser, Wolfgang. "Samuel Beckett's Dramatic Language." *Modern Drama*, 9, No. 3 (Dec. 1966), 251–59.

Jacobsen, Josephine and Mueller, William R. *The Testament of Samuel Beckett*. New York: Hill & Wang, 1964.

Janvier, Ludovic. *Beckett par lui-même*. Paris: Amateurs de Livres (Ecrivains de Toujours, No. 83).

———. *Pour Samuel Beckett*. Paris: Les Editions de Minuit, 1966.

Kain, Richard M. "The Limits of Literary Interpretation." *Journal of Aesthetics and Art Criticism*, 17, No. 2 (Dec. 1958), 214–18.

Karl, Frederick R. "Pursuit of the Real." *The Nation*, 194, No. 16 (21 April 1962), 345–49.

Kazin, Alfred. "The Literary Mind." *The Nation*, 200, No. 8 (20 Sept. 1965), 203–06.

Keawitter, Robert. "Being and Time in Samuel Beckett's Novels." *Dissertation Abstracts*, 26 (June 1966), 7320.

Kenner, Hugh. "Beckett, the Rational Domain." *Forum*, 3 (Summer 1960), 39–47.

———. *Flaubert, Joyce and Beckett, the Stoic Comedians*. Boston: Beacon Press, 1962.

Kern, Edith. "Beckett and the Spirit of the Commedia dell'arte." *Modern Drama*, 9, No. 3 (Dec. 1966), 260–67.

———. "Beckett's Knight of Infinite Resignation." *Yale French Studies*, 29 (1962), 49–56.

———. "Drama Stripped for Inaction." *Yale French Studies* (Today's French Theatre), 14 (1954–1955), 41–47.

———. *Existential Thought and Fictional Technique: Kierkegaard, Sartre, Beckett*. New Haven: Yale University Press, 1970.

Kleppner, Amy M. "Philosophy and the Literary Medium: The Existentialist Predicament." *Journal of Aesthetics and Art Criticism*, 23, No. 2 (Winter 1965), 207–17.

Kott, Jan. "A note on Beckett's realism." *The Tulane Drama Review*, 10, No. 3 (Spring 1960), 156–59.

Lamont, Rosette. "The Metaphysical Farce." *French Review*, 32, No. 4 (Feb. 1959), 319–28.

Le Hardouin, Maria. "L'Anti-Héros ou 'Richard n'aime plus Richard.' " *Synthèses* (Brussels), 12ᵉ année, No. 139 (Dec. 1957), 398–405.

Lewis, John. "Samuel Beckett and the Decline of Western Civilization." *Marxism Today*, 8, No. 12 (Dec. 1964), 381–84.

Macksey, Richard. "The Artist and the Labyrinth: Design or *Dasein*." *Modern Language Notes*, 77, No. 3 (May 1962), 239–56.

Marcel, Gabriel. "Atomisation du théâtre." *Nouvelles Littéraires, Artistiques et Scientifiques*, No. 1555 (June 1957), 10.

Margolis, Joseph, ed. *Philosophy Looks at The Arts*. New York: Charles Scribner's Sons, 1962.

Marissel, André. *Beckett*. Paris: Classiques du XXe siècle, Editions Universitaires, 1963.

Mayoux, J.-J. "Beckett and Expressionism." *Modern Drama*, 9, No. 3 (Dec. 1966), 238–41.

———. "Samuel Beckett et l'univers parodique." *Les Lettres Nouvelles*, No. 6 (Aug. 1960), 271–91.

Mélèse, Pierre. *Samuel Beckett*. Paris: Seghers, 1966.

Mendes, João. "Vida Literária." *Brotéria, Série Mensal Sciencias-Letras*, 69 (1959), 57–68.

Milhalyi, Gabor. "Beckett's 'Godot' and the Myth of Alienation." *Modern Drama*, 9, No. 3 (Dec. 1966), 277–82.

Molière, J.-B.-P. *Oeuvres complètes*, II. Ed. Maurice Rat. Paris: n.p., 1956.

Morgan, Douglas N. "Must Art Tell the Truth?" *Journal of Aesthetics and Art Criticism*, 26, No. 1 (Fall 1967), 17–27.

Morse, Mitchell J. "The Contemplative Life According to S. Beckett." *Hudson Review*, 15, No. 4 (Winter 1962–1963), 512–24.

Mueller, Gustav E. "Philosophy in the Twentieth Century American Novel." *Journal of Aesthetics and Art Criticism*, 16, No. 4 (June 1958), 471–81.

Nadeau, Maurice. "Beckett, la tragédie transposée en farce." *Avant Scène* (Paris), No. 156 (1957), 4–6.

Noon, William T. "Modern Literature and the Sense of Time." *Thought*, 33, No. 131 (Winter 1958–1959), 571–603.

Nores, Dominique. "La Condition humaine selon Beckett." *Théâtre d'Aujourd'hui*, No. 3 (Sept.–Oct. 1957), 9–12.

North, Robert J. *Myth in the Modern French Theatre*. Keele, Eng.: University of Keele, 1962.

Oberg, Arthur. "Krapp's Last Tape and the Proustian Vision." *Modern Drama*, 9, No. 3 (Dec. 1966), 333–38.

O'Brien, Justin. "Samuel Beckett and André Gide: an Hypothesis." *French Review*, Feb. 1967, 485–86.

Onimus, Jean. *Beckett*. (Series, Les Ecrivains devant Dieu). Paris: Desclée de Brouwer, 1968.

———. "L'homme égaré." *Etudes*, 283, No. 13 (Dec. 1954), 320–29.

————. "Samuel Beckett, le clochard et l'asile." *Revue Générale Belge*, No. 11 (1968), 5–17.

Pauly, Herta. "The Autonomy of Art: Fact or Norm?" *Journal of Aesthetics and Art Criticism*, 18, No. 2 (Dec. 1959), 204–14.

Pouillon, Jean. "Une morale de la conscience absolue." *Les Temps Modernes*, July 1951, 283–86.

Pronko, Leonard. "Beckett, Ionesco, Schehadé: The Avant-Garde Theatre." *Modern Language Forum*, 42 (1958), 118–23.

Radke, Judith J. "The Theater of Samuel Beckett: 'Une Durée à Animer'." *Yale French Studies*, 29 (1962), 57–64.

Rechtien, John. "Time and Eternity Meet in the Present." *Texas Studies in Literature and Language*, 6, No. 1 (Spring 1964), 5–21.

Reichert, John F. "Description and Interpretation in Literary Criticism." *Journal of Aesthetics and Art Criticism*, 27, No. 3 (Spring 1969), 281–92.

Reid, Alec. "Beckett and the Drama of Unknowing." *Drama Survey*, 2, No. 2 (Fall 1962), 130–38.

Rexroth, Kenneth. "The Point of Irrelevance." *The Nation*, 182, No. 15 (14 Apr. 1956), 325–28.

Rickels, Milton. "Existential Themes in Beckett's 'Unnamable'." *Criticism*, 4, No. 2 (Spring 1962), 134–47.

Rosbo, Patrick de. "Le Théâtre et la mort." *Cahiers du Théâtre*, 2ᵉ année, No. 3 (1–2ᵉ trim. 1965), 26–35.

Rosen, Stanley. *Nihilism, A Philosophical Essay*. New Haven: Yale University Press, 1969.

Ross, Stephen D. *Literature and Philosophy*. New York: Appleton-Century-Crofts, 1969.

Schechner, Richard. "There's Lots of Time in Godot." *Modern Drama*, 9, No. 3 (Dec. 1966), 268–76. (Also in R. Cohn's *Casebook*, 175 ff.)

Schipper, Edith Watson. "The Wisdom of Tragedy." *Journal of Aesthetics and Art Criticism*, 24, No. 4 (Summer 1966), 533–37.

Schneider, Daniel J. "Techniques of Cognition in Modern Fiction." *Journal of Aesthetics and Art Criticism*, 26, No. 3 (Spring 1968), 317–28.

Schoeck, Richard J. "Mathematics and the Languages of Literary Criticism." *Journal of Aesthetics and Art Criticism*, 26, No. 3 (Spring 1968), 367–76.

Scott, Nathan A. *Samuel Beckett*. London: Bowes & Bows, 1965.

Skulsky, Harold. "Literature and Philosophy: The Common Ground." *Journal of Aesthetics and Art Criticism*, 27, No. 2 (Winter 1968), 183–97.

Sparshott, F. E. "Truth in Fiction." *Journal of Aesthetics and Art Criticism*,

26, No. 1 (Fall 1967), 3–7.

Stolnitz, Jerome. "Notes on Comedy and Tragedy." *Philosophy and Phenomenological Research*, 16 (Sept. 1955), 45–60.

Stratford, Philip. "Creativity and Commitment in Contemporary Theatre." *Humanities Association of Canada Bulletin*, 15, No. 2 (Autumn 1964), 35–39.

Sypher, Wylie. *Loss of the Self in Modern Literature and Art*. New York: Random House, Inc., 1962.

Teilhard de Chardin, Pierre. *L'Avenir de l'homme*. Paris: Editions du Seuil, 1959.

Thiher, Allen. "*Le Maître de Santiago* and Tragic Affirmation." *Romance Notes*, 11, No. 2 (Winter 1969), 238–43.

Thompson, William I. "Freedom and Comedy." *Tulane Drama Review*, 9, No. 3 (Spring 1965), 216–30.

Touchard, Pierre-Aimé. "Le Théâtre de Samuel Beckett." *Revue de Paris*, 68ᵉ année, No. 2 (Feb. 1961), 73–87.

———. "Un Théâtre nouveau." *Avant Scène* (Paris), No. 156 (1957), 1–2.

Viatte, Auguste. "La Littérature dans l'impasse." *La Revue de l'Université Laval*, 15, No. 3 (Nov. 1960), 254–59.

Walsh, Dorothy. "The Cognitive Content of Art." *The Problems of Aesthetics*. Ed. Eliseo Vivas and Murray Krieger. New York: Holt, Rinehart & Winston, 1965.

Warnock, G. J. *English Philosophy Since 1900*. New York: Oxford University Press, 1966.

Webner, Hélène. "Waiting for Godot and the New Theology." *Renasence*, 21, 3–9, 31.

Weitz, Morris. *Hamlet and the Philosophy of Literary Criticism*. New York: World Publishing Company, 1966.

———. *Philosophy in Literature*. Detroit: Wayne State University Press, 1963.

———. *Philosophy of the Arts*. Cambridge: Harvard University Press, 1950.

Wellworth, G. E. "Life in The Void: Samuel Beckett." *University* [of Kansas City] *Review*, 28 (1961), 25–33.

Wendler, Herbert W. "Graveyard Humanism." *Southwest Review*, 49, No. 1 (Winter 1964), 44–52.

Wilder, Amos N. "Mortality and Contemporary Literature." *Harvard Theological Review*, 58, No. 1 (Jan. 1965), 1–20.

Williams, Raymond. *Modern Tragedy*. Stanford: Stanford University Press, 1966.

Wilson, Robert N. "Samuel Beckett and The Social Psychology of Emptiness." *Journal of Social Issues* (Jan. 1964), 62–70.

Wittgenstein, Ludwig. *Philosophical Investigations*. New York: The Macmillan Company, 1953.

————. *Tractatus Logico-Philosophicus*. London: Routledge & Kegan Paul, Ltd., 1922.

Yerlès, Pierre. "Le Théâtre de Samuel Beckett." *La Revue Nouvelle*, 33, No. 4 (Apr. 1961), 401–07.

Zink, Sidney. "The Novel as a Medium of Modern Tragedy." *Journal of Aesthetics and Art Criticism*, 17, No. 2 (Dec. 1958), 169–73.

INDEX